THE (Incredibly Useful) BOOK OF DELEGATION

HOW TO DELEGATE SO IT GETS DONE CORRECTLY THE FIRST TIME!

Silver Rose, CCS

THE (Incredibly Useful) BOOK OF DELEGATION

Printed by CreateSpace.com
Printed in the USA
ISBN-10: 1973721503
ISBN-13: 978-1973721505

CreateSpace Independent Publishing Platform
North Charleston, South Carolina

Silver Rose
The (Incredibly Useful) Book of Delegation, How to Delegate So It Gets Done Correctly The First Time!

Info@SilverSpeaks.com

Incredibly Useful
THE BOOK OF DELEGATION

Dedication

To—

the many clients over the years whose trust in me has been humbling and gratifying at the same time. Much of what is in this book I learned from working with you

Ann Ewen, Ph.D., Strategic Advisor to CEO's at Vistage International who originally gave me the idea for this book

Tracy Penwell, friend and coach who wouldn't let me give up on the Socratic Delegation concept

Nancy Lockwood whose input was, and always is, invaluable

Always To—

my beloved Bill Jurika who, although gone, sits on my shoulder every day and says, "Good for you, honey!"

my daughters Promise and Shadow's Tears whose daily courage takes my breath away

and Nancy Lindsey whose friendship means everything

Incredibly Useful
THE BOOK OF DELEGATION

CONTENTS

Incredibly Useful
THE BOOK OF DELEGATION

WHY I WROTE THIS ^{Incredibly Useful} BOOK

When I left the corporate world to start my business, I was primarily a life coach. My singular focus was how to live a happy life, an expertise I had acquired while overcoming a clinical depression that began in early childhood and was lifted 30 years later.

Some people scoff at our society's seemingly incessant drive for happiness. To them I say, "Think about any one thing you desire. Don't you want it because you think that when you get it you'll be happier?" Whether it's a new car, a new love, or a new job, the end goal for any acquisition is to feel better.

In my coaching practice, I soon noticed that one barrier to happiness seemed to crop up in nearly every one of my clients—having a job they looked forward to. I also began to notice that the degree to which someone was engaged in their work (and therefore looked forward to doing it) had quite a lot to do with their relationship with their immediate supervisor.

It turns out I'm not the only one to notice. Countless books, polls, workshops, podcasts, blogs, seminars, and Ted Talks have been devoted to Employee Engagement and how leaders need to behave to get their teams on board.

I decided to expand my coaching practice. I began developing programs related to improving Employee Engagement. As I researched this topic, I saw a lot of high-level philosophy about leadership, employee benefits and perks, and team building. What I didn't see was much discourse about the direct correlation between Employee Engagement and these three areas:

1. Delegation
2. Feedback
3. Laughter in the workplace

As it turns out, one of the most significant obstacles to enjoying work is a lack of delegation skills. Too many supervisors, managers, and executives simply don't know how to delegate in a way that empowers. They give orders, cleverly disguised as instructions or requests instead of empowering their team members to develop solutions on their own. This is why I decided to focus my first *Incredibly Useful* book on this important topic. Feedback and Laughter in the Workplace will be covered in future *Incredibly Useful* books.

As part of my research, I talked with executive coaches, most working only at the C-Suite level. To a person, they confided in me that every leader *thinks* s/he knows how to delegate and most of them are abysmal at it. One coach whose clientele are all senior level attorneys implored, "Teach them the difference between delegating and dumping!"

To get good at delegation, you have to completely overhaul how you think about and approach leadership. Your organization has to live it and breathe it every day until it becomes ingrained. You must continually ask, "Am I leading or commanding?" In order to lead, you have to let go of your ego that so desperately wants to command.

I'm not kidding when I say it's all about empowering others. This requires the courage to give up tight control.

I wrote this book to teach those of you in leadership specifically how to get your teams to strategize, take ownership of the work, and be accountable for their results—all key aspects of Employee Engagement.

Over the years I have had the pleasure of working with hundreds of leaders from supervisors to CEOs to public sector leadership. As they let go of their old habits of "command and control" and learned how to delegate, they got significantly more productivity out of their teams. That looks great on a spreadsheet but more importantly, their employees are much happier and more engaged.

They learned what I hope you will discover as you apply the principles of this book: ***an engaged team makes work a dream.***

Acknowledgments

It is the vanity of many writers who believe they can edit their own work; I am no exception. Thankfully, reason overcame ego, and I turned to others for help. They were gracious enough to give of their precious time to read my manuscript and give me notes for improvement. My sincere thanks go to Nancy Fredericks, Kathy Richards, and Nancy Lockwood. Because of you, I have more confidence in the message of this book.

Barbara McNichol of Barbara McNichol Editorial patiently put up with having many cooks in this particular kitchen and gave me a professionally polished manuscript. Your talent is only exceeded by your graciousness.

And my deep appreciation for Brooke Simmons, graphic designer at Fiverr. com who diligently and patiently worked with me on the layout of this book.

WHAT YOU WILL LEARN IN THIS ⌣Incredibly Useful BOOK

About Leadership

- Why your instructions aren't being carried out correctly and what you can do about it
- How to replace one-sided delegation with collaborative conversations
- When command-and-control leadership is necessary and appropriate
- How to employ specific techniques to empower your team
- How to use a simple listening process that instills trust and inspires action
- How to get more productivity from the team you have

About Talent Development

- Ways to delegate that empower your team to take ownership of their roles
- Tools to uncover the thought processes of your team members as they relate to deliverables
- How and why to develop an in-depth understanding of each staff member's capabilities
- How to develop your employees' competencies, knowledge, and skills through delegation
- How to get your team members to think for themselves

WHY YOU SHOULD READ THIS ⌄Incredibly Useful BOOK

The phrase "publish or perish" has been coined to describe the pressure in academia to continually publish academic work to sustain or advance one's career. The equivalent phrase in organizations would be **"delegate or disintegrate."**

Dramatic? Perhaps—but also true.

When leaders within an organization don't know the subtleties required for developing influence by delegating well, this lack of skill has a dramatic effect on employee engagement and ultimately the organization's bottom line. Over time, the organization slowly disintegrates like the damage caused by water continuously dripping on a rock.

At the beginning of my leadership programs, I ask attendees this question: If I could reveal the answer to one issue around the topic of leading others, what would that issue be?

Typically, on the topic of delegation, I hear a version of one of the following:

- I work hard to give good directions. Why aren't they carried out correctly?
- Why do so few people think for themselves?
- How can I inspire my team to take action?
- How do I get others to WANT to take action?
- How do we get Millennials working for us, not just for themselves?

This book contains answers to those questions and more.

No matter the level, if you're already a leader in your organization or strive to become one, it's a safe bet you struggle with delegating effectively. You can always get those who report to you to "obey," but inspiring them to collaborate is the sweet spot of leadership.

Learning how to delegate well ultimately leads to increased employee engagement. Here are some cold, hard facts about why you should care:

> "The #1 leadership skill that halts company growth is an inability to delegate." — Jim Alampi, author, *Great to Excellent; It's the Execution!*

- Poll after poll reveals the #1 concern of small to midsize businesses is how to grow revenue.

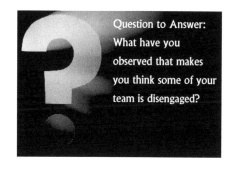

Question to Answer: What have you observed that makes you think some of your team is disengaged?

• The equivalent concern in nonprofit and public sector organizations is cutting costs and doing more with less.

• According to the most recent Gallup poll on the topic, 67.5% of your employees are disengaged (and so is 65% of your leadership team!).

• A study by payroll giant ADP puts the financial cost of each disengaged employee at $2,634 a year. Most organizational development professionals say they believe the cost to be significantly higher. $2,634 is an average and depends on employees' salaries and benefits. The higher the disengaged employee's compensation, the more it is costing your organization.

• In real dollars and cents, this means that for every 100 employees you have, 67.5 are disengaged, costing your company a minimum of $177,795 a year (67.5 X $2,634).

Here are a few things you could use $177,795 for:

o A new Maserati

o A Bavaria 36-foot sailboat

o Two to four new employees

Do the Math for Your Organization

Grab your calculator or smartphone and figure it out. Take your total

number of employees, multiply by 67.5%, and then multiply that result by $2,634.

Fill in your answer below:

Employee disengagement is costing my organization $_____/year.

To drive the point home even further, take the total number of people on your management team (all levels) and multiply by 65%, which is the percentage of managers that Gallup found to be disengaged. Common sense says the actual cost, although not separately calculated, has to be even higher than that number.

Gallup also revealed that 15.7% of the employee population is "actively disengaged." The difference between a disengaged employee and an employee who is "actively disengaged" can be viewed as the difference between ambivalence and sabotage—that is, taking action to ruin something.

How can leaders combat both ambivalence and sabotage? An essential component for getting employees engaged and more willing to bring the best of themselves to work each day is collaborative leadership.

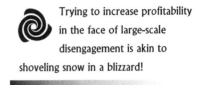

Trying to increase profitability in the face of large-scale disengagement is akin to shoveling snow in a blizzard!

Success in leading others to act depends on whether you are a "command-and-control boss" or a "collaborative leader." What's the difference?

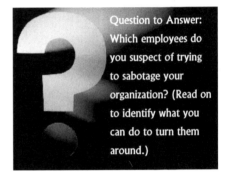

Question to Answer: Which employees do you suspect of trying to sabotage your organization? (Read on to identify what you can do to turn them around.)

When delegating, a "**command-and-control boss**" tends to do some or all of the following:

• Issues orders and expects them to be followed to the letter. When they're not, s/he becomes incredibly frustrated.

• Focuses on the employees' shortcomings, delegates in spite of them, and micro-manages them.

• Asks the employees' input on a task to be delegated and then callously overrides it.

• Issues orders/directions as a primary style of delegation

By comparison, a "**collaborative leader**" delegates by:

• Telling employees the desired outcome and then brainstorms with them how to get it done and/or encourages them to come back with a solution they've developed on their own.

• Focusing on the employees' capabilities and delegates with confidence and trust.

"A good leader leads the people from above them. A great leader leads the people from within them. "
— M.D. Arnold

• Endorsing rather than overriding an employee's approach. S/he works with the employee to reach a mutual agreement on how to move forward.

• Using a delegation style of "together we solve problems."

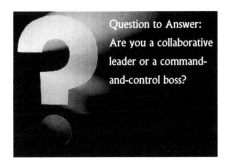

Question to Answer: Are you a collaborative leader or a command-and-control boss?

Answering this question isn't as simple as it might seem. Likely, you're a mix of the two. Some days, you happily collaborate with your team. Others days—usually during a time crunch—you revert to a command-and-control style. This book provides you with the tools you need to primarily be a "collaborative leader." Read on!

Which Generation is Least Engaged?

According to Gallup's research, which generation makes up the least engaged employees? Millennials at 29%. (The Pew Research Center, an American think tank, defines "adult Millennials" as being born between 1981 and 1996.)

When it comes to getting people to do what needs to be done at work, are Millennials so different than employees of other generations? It's a hotly debated topic in workplaces everywhere. Here's the biggest difference I see. I was raised by post-World War II parents who rarely showed the slightest interest in my opinions. Millennials, on the other hand, were raised by parents who over-corrected in this area. Growing up, this generation got to weigh in on everything in the family. Their parents listened to them in a way that my generation's parents had little patience for.

Not only that, but Millennials primarily have Baby Boomer parents (born between 1946 and 1964 according to the Pew Research Center) who were intimidated by all the technology flooding into their homes. While the parents of these Baby Boomers often said, "Children should be seen and not heard," parents of Millennials *encouraged* them to talk. In fact, as children, Millennials often became the unofficial "tech support team" within the family. As a result, they received a lot of positive feedback: "Oh, honey. I could NEVER have figured that out. You're a genius!"

Admit it! If a new piece of technology causes you problems and someone (no matter the age) resolves the issues for you, don't you want to embrace them with tears of gratitude?

Picking up the tools and following the techniques in this book will go a long way toward engaging ALL generations of employees including Millennials and the generation that follows. Know that most Millennials want to work, learn, contribute, and be heard; the big differentiator is they want to have a good time doing it. They clearly remember their parents dragging themselves home from work each day complaining about the job and they swore, "That will never happen to me." Millennials are eager to be asked for help—this is what motivates them—and they will jump in as they did for their parents. But giving them orders simply won't work. Fortunately, you're about to learn a different approach.

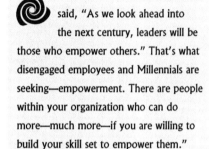 Microsoft Founder Bill Gates has said, "As we look ahead into the next century, leaders will be those who empower others." That's what disengaged employees and Millennials are seeking—empowerment. There are people within your organization who can do more—much more—if you are willing to build your skill set to empower them."

Empowering means creating an environment in which team members are encouraged to explore better ways to do the work, develop strategies rather than waiting for solutions to be given to them, and take ownership of results.

This book will help you to learn how.

---

http://www.gallup.com/poll/189071/little-change-employee-engagement-january.aspx
http://www.gallup.com/businessjournal/182228/managers-engaged-jobs.aspx
http://www.gallup.com/poll/189071/little-change-employee-engagement-january.aspx
http://www.gallup.com/businessjournal/195209/few-millennials-engaged-work.aspx
http://www.pewresearch.org/fact-tank/2015/03/19/how-millennials-compare-with-their-grandparents/

"Would I rather be feared or loved? Easy. Both. I want people to be afraid of how much they love me."

-Michael Scott, The Office

CHAPTER 1: INTRODUCING THE DELEGATION PROCESS FOR TODAY'S WORLD

A critical component of leadership is to understand the core competencies and capacity of your team. Delegating effectively ensures you know the answers to the following four questions, and more.

Do you:

1. Know how each of your team members thinks about and approaches his/her work?
2. Have an in-depth understanding of each team member's capabilities?
3. Know what energizes each team member?
4. Know how to empower your whole team?

Master the Art of Asking Questions

One sage answer to the oft-asked question,"How do I delegate so my instructions are carried out correctly?" has its roots far back in history to 46-399 BC, the time of the Greek philosopher Socrates.

What in the world does a Greek philosopher have to do with leadership and delegation? It's this: Socrates developed a way of teaching that involves asking questions to stimulate others to come up with their own reasoning, solutions, and answers. Isn't that what you want when you ask, "Why can't people think for themselves?" You want them to come up with their own reasoning, solutions, and answers!

Today's personal and executive coaching methodologies are deeply entrenched in what's known as the Socratic Method. In fact, coaching is rooted in the concept that an individual has all the internal resources necessary to succeed. A coach simply speeds up the process by posing questions that, when answered by the person, lead to action that gets him/her to succeed more quickly than they would without coaching.

It turns out the Socratic Method is also an excellent model for effective delegation. Leaders at those rare organizations with high employee engagement have enthusiastically adopted it.

Say Hello to Socratic Delegation

A key skill for leaders today is the ability to ask questions and draw out answers from others—the Socratic Method.

How can you apply the Socratic Method to build your leadership skills as well as the capacity and energy of your team? By asking the right questions when assigning tasks and projects. Called Socratic Delegation, here's how it works: when delegating, instead of telling your employee how to perform the task, clearly delineate the results you need, then ask, "What are some ways to get this done?"

> "I cannot teach anybody anything. I can only make them think."
>
> — Socrates,
> Greek philosopher
> (469-399 BCE)

What happens? You get more of what you focus on and **questions guide focus.** They shift the delegation conversation from, "I'm the mighty and all powerful Oz so let me tell you how to do it" to "This is your wheelhouse so how do you suggest we approach it?" The former focuses on you as the expert, the latter on the knowledge of the person who owns that area of responsibility or process.

Socratic Delegation invites each person to SOAR

<u>St</u>rategy

<u>O</u>wnership

<u>A</u>ccountability

<u>R</u>esults

THE _{Incredibly Useful} SOCRATIC DELEGATION PROCESS STEP-BY-STEP

Step #1 - Identify the task or project.

Step #2 - Clearly state the measurable results/outcomes and timeframe. (By the way, this is often the culprit of problems. If you don't clearly define how to measure success, how is the person to whom you are delegating supposed to know?)

Step #3 - Meet with the individual or team to whom you are delegating and have the following conversation:

- "Here's an overview of the work and why it needs to be done." The why of what you're delegating is very important. People are more likely to become engaged in their work if they know why they're doing it. Millennials in particular want to understand why.
- "Here is the result needed and the date we need it: _____."
- "Would you walk me through how you think it should be done?" OR "How do you think we should approach this?"
- Listen and only listen until the end. Take notes so you remember the agreements made.
- Don't interrupt; if you identify a problem and stop to mention it, you may interrupt the person's thought process. Also, it's likely s/he will, while talking through the task, identify the very problem you noticed and address it directly—the ideal scenario.

Step # 4 - Fine-tune

- If you noticed any potential concerns while the plans were being outlined, bring them up by asking questions:

- ◊ How will you get to that point?
- ◊ Where are those resources coming from?
- ◊ Help me understand _____
- ◊ What tools are you planning to use?
- ◊ What obstacles might stand in the way of getting this done on time?
- ◊ And so on.

- This fine-tuning process is your opportunity to coach the individual to a higher level of skill and strategizing.
- This is also an opportunity for you to learn approaches you hadn't thought of yourself.
- It gives you a perfect chance to acknowledge the team or individual for thinking critically.
- Before delegating to any member of your team, be certain YOU are clear about Steps 1 and 2:
  1. Identify the task or project, and
  2. Clearly state the measurable results/outcomes and timeframe.

Each step is critical to achieving success.

For a PDF of the Socratic Delegation Process, go to:
http://www.DelegateForResults.com/SocraticDelegationProcess

If your goals include increasing performance and employee engagement (and they should), involving your team members in planning how a task or project might be done is a simple, powerful way to achieve those goals. Utilizing the Step-by-Step Socratic Delegation Process will go a long way toward achieving exactly that.

What Actually Happens While You're Giving Instructions

> Insider Tip:
> Never ask for "the best approach" or "the solution" as if only one exists. When people think there's only one correct answer, they freeze, fearing their first answer will be incorrect. This is when they implore, "Just tell me what to do and I'll do it," because they're afraid to get it wrong. People problem-solve more effectively when they're asked for potential solutions or approaches (plural).

Just for a moment, think of a time your boss or, if you're the CEO, your biggest customer made a request for a deliverable. Now quickly answer this question: the very second you understood what was being requested, what began to happen in your mind?

That's right! You started to plan how you'd fulfill the request. And while you were making plans in your head, the requestor continued to talk, explaining what s/he wanted in full detail. That person, if a fan of command-and-control, might even have given you the exact steps to take. But you weren't fully listening, were you? That's because, in your mind, you were already in full-blown, project-planning mode.

This is precisely what happens when you delegate to your team members. The moment they think they grasp what you want, their minds get busy making plans. While they're doing that, they're not closely listening to your instructions and the rest of the conversation. The only shot you have at getting your request fulfilled properly is to find out what your team member is planning.

What plan is being formulated inside your team member's head as you are giving instructions? Find out!

Socrates: Meet Mr. Spock!

Would you like to have the ability to figure out what someone else is planning to do? Would that be useful? I don't mean the ability to read minds. I think we can all agree—THAT particular super power could take us places we don't want to go. No, reading someone's mind could be trouble, but knowing what someone is planning as it relates to what you're delegating has value. If you agree, you'll appreciate what I'm about to reveal. It's a key component of the Socratic Method and successful delegation.

I am a huge Star Trek fan. If you've seen the TV show or any of the movies, you might recall that Mr. Spock, who was a Vulcan as opposed to an Earthling, had the ability to merge his mind with the essence of another's mind. It was called the Vulcan Mind Meld. Unfortunately, we're not Vulcans so we cannot do the Vulcan Mind Meld.

Or can we?

I'm about to reveal the secret of doing the Earthling version of the Vulcan Mind Meld. I call it The Delegation Mind Meld.

The author with Mr. Spock

Here's how to find out how your team members plan to execute on the tasks/projects you're delegating. You ready? Drum roll, please.

ASK THEM!

And I don't mean ask, "What are you thinking right now?" Asking that question can throw someone into a complete panic. They're frantically wondering, "Do you mean what am I thinking now, or what was I thinking when you asked me? What are you hoping I'll say? Is there a right answer for this or am I doomed no matter how I answer? Is this a trap? Is my job on the line? Honestly, I don't even remember what I was thinking when you asked me because I'm trying to figure out what you want me to say!" (Take a breath!)

Because your team members start planning how to tackle tasks the moment you tell them what you want, it's critically important to identify the outcome you want and then say a version of this: "Walk me through how you

Learning how each individual on your team thinks about work is crucial on many levels. If you tell them how to carry out their assignments (command-and-control), the only data point you have for what they're capable of is what you can observe. If instead you use Socratic Delegation, you will learn how they think and develop strategies. It's entirely possible that right now you have at least one team member who could be an asset in other areas if you only knew the persons level of sophistication when it comes to planning.

think we should do it." The answer will give you access to what each team member is planning.

When individuals reveal their plans to you, you're doing the Delegation Mind Meld! Suddenly, you have access to how they're planning to execute the task or project. At that point, you can determine whether it will likely give you the desired result or if it requires tweaking. You will also begin to develop a deeper understanding of how they think about and approach work. The more you understand this, the better you can take full advantage of their competencies and talents.

As you listen to each team member outlining the plan, you might suddenly realize you forgot to impart a key piece of information. Provide the new data and then ask for ideas in light of the new information. If his/her plan still doesn't meet with your approval, ask these follow-up questions:

- What other approaches might work?
- What could go wrong with that plan?
- How do you know that Department B will be able to give us what we need in time to execute your plan?

(See Deep Socratic Delegation at the end of this book for comprehensive lists of questions to ask.)

Why is the Delegation Mind Meld So Effective?

Admit it, aren't you crazy about your own ideas? Aren't you motivated to execute them? So, too, are your team members eager to implement their ideas.

Allow Them to Formulate and Implement Their Own Ideas. What's the ultimate goal of the Delegation Mind Meld? You want those to whom you're delegating to walk away with a plan for execution that you fully endorse and that they believe was completely their own idea. If your team members think something was their idea in the first place, what are the odds the plan will be done as agreed? YES, close to 100%! This is because when they voice their plan to you, they're fully involved. They'll remember what was agreed to, and they'll do it.

Sounds simple, right? It is, but it's not easy.

We love giving unsolicited advice. We love offering unsolicited opinions. We love providing unsolicited anything because we hear—and LOVE—the sound of our own voices. Nowhere is this more evident than when delegating.

When you answer a question they never asked, here's what people hear: BLAH BLAH BLAH BLAH BLAH BLAH. So if you're a do-gooder sprinkling your fairy dust of brilliant ideas all over the planet (or at least the workplace), you can stop now. NO ONE'S LISTENING. Haven't you suspected that all along?

If you were taught to believe answers are more important than questions, think back to your school days. Who were the teachers you found most engaging—those who lectured or those who engaged you by asking questions?

As a leader, you'll find the Delegation Mind Meld has tremendous value. How much easier would your work be if you asked questions of people who have the answers instead of always having to be the one with the answers? And how much easier would life be if your team members delivered the results you requested the first time, every time?

> "An answer to a question no one asked is a wasted answer."
>
> —Esther Hicks,
> author, lecturer on Law of Attraction

What's a quick, effortless way to achieve the Delegation Mind Meld? Use the process of Socratic Delegation.

I can almost hear your groans. "Silver, if I have to do this every time, there won't be time left for anything to get done! We'll be *talking* about work instead of *doing* it!" Fear not. I assure you that, as you practice this new style of delegation, it will get quicker and there will be shortcuts, a sort of "secret language" of delegation. Once your team gets used to it, you'll be able to present the outcome and then say, "Walk me through your approach."

 The more you are aware of how your team members think — how they plan to carry out the tasks and projects you assign them — the more you can influence the end results.

Initially, it will be like learning a new app—awkward and time-consuming at first—but once mastered, you don't know how you lived without it!

The "Secret Sauce" that Makes Socratic Delegation Work

Allow me to reveal the most powerful skill anyone who wants influence MUST master: once you ask a question,

SHUT UP!

Or stated more politely, **STOP TALKING, PRACTICE SILENCE, and LISTEN.**

This powerful technique is taught in all the top executive negotiation and sales courses, and yet we fail to use it where it can make

 If you are reluctant to learn Socratic Delegation, ponder this question: Why is it that we never seem to have time to make plans in advance but we always have time to fix things when they go wrong? Over time (and I'm talking about as short a time as a month), using this process will save countless hours of fixing mistakes that could have been avoided.

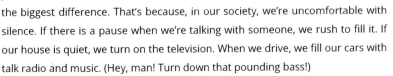

the biggest difference. That's because, in our society, we're uncomfortable with silence. If there is a pause when we're talking with someone, we rush to fill it. If our house is quiet, we turn on the television. When we drive, we fill our cars with talk radio and music. (Hey, man! Turn down that pounding bass!)

To become an influential leader, practice silence until you get comfortable with it. This skill will serve you well. You'll gain a reputation for being a good listener, having incredible wisdom, and eliciting exceptional performance from your team—all without saying a word. Instead, invoke the 80/20 rule.

Deafening Sounds of Silence

Are you uncomfortable with gaps in conversation? Do you find yourself saying something, anything, to fill the silence? Do you try to "help" by suggesting possible answers to the question you just asked? In a courtroom, this would be met with an objection from opposing counsel to the judge, "Your Honor, my colleague is leading the witness with these questions." How often do you find yourself doing the same thing, perhaps with some arrogance?

In our society, people no longer allow others enough time to ruminate. They expect ready answers and become uncomfortable when they're not offered. If silence hangs, our minds race as we wonder what the other person is thinking or how she is reacting. Is she mad at me? Have I offended her? How do I fix this? If our questions aren't answered quickly, we step in and offer suggestions for what the answers might be under the guise of being compassionate or helpful.

 The 80/20 Rule of Delegation Conversations: You'll know you're having a successful interaction if you're doing 20% of the talking by asking clarifying questions, and your team member is doing 80% of the talking by providing input.

In fact, though, we're being phenomenally rude.

Most people are silent because they are thinking. Some think fast and respond quickly while others take their time, carefully choosing their words. So don't insist that your team members think for themselves and then rush them through the process!

When you ask someone a question and then jump in impatiently to supply the answer, you have just told that person, "Clearly you are too stupid to answer for yourself, so allow me, with my superior intelligence and experience, to help you."

The Power of "The Gap" in Socratic Delegation

If, during the silence, you wait with genuine curiosity to hear the response to your question, then you are in the mode of discovery, and the person with whom you're interacting won't feel intimidated. If, however, you've already decided what you hope the response will be, then you are, once again, "leading the witness" and causing discomfort.

Said in a different way, if you are genuinely curious about what the other person comes up with, this is called coaching, and it's powerful. When you're hoping they will offer your solution, you are controlling, and that's unpleasant.

I learned about the power of the gap while studying to be an executive coach. The art of coaching consists of asking questions designed to stimulate others' thinking so they can develop their own conclusions and solutions—not yours! That formulation of solutions happens during the gap.

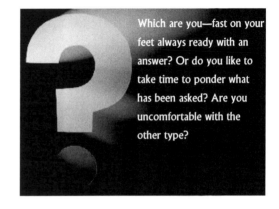

Which are you—fast on your feet always ready with an answer? Or do you like to take time to ponder what has been asked? Are you uncomfortable with the other type?

Your job? Get more comfortable with the gap. After you've asked someone a question, see if you can sit quietly and be curious to hear the response. When silence falls between you, wonder about these questions while you wait:

- What will he say?
- Does he know more about this than I know?
- Will he come up with something I never thought of?

When you let the power of the gap unfold, you'll discover two things:

1. Those around you are smarter than you knew; and
2. If you're open-minded enough to admit #1, you may learn something.

Good conversations, especially those within the context of work, are collaborative. Ideas are exchanged. Within the richest exchanges, a gap between the question asked and the response given shows up. This gap sounds like silence, yet a wealth of information is born within it. If you rush the dialogue by filling in the answers, you'll miss giving birth to important ideas. That's why the gap is often referred to as a "pregnant pause."

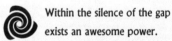

Within the silence of the gap exists an awesome power.

To tap into it doesn't simply require you to sit and wait. It requires you to sit, wait, and be curious.

Six Basic Questions

If you haven't already, you will soon notice that the elements of the questions used in Socratic Delegation look suspiciously like the questions taught in journalism class about writing a good story.

These six words — who, what, when, where, why and how — provide excellent beginnings for delegation questions because they can't be answered "yes" or "no." Instead, they require thoughtful consideration and stimulate dialogue.

Note: The questions at the back of this book in Deeper Socratic Delegation all use one of these six questions as their beginning.

Conclusion ->

Whether you are a C-Suite executive, a frontline supervisor, or a project manager, an effective way to decrease costs and increase revenues in your organization is to use the Socratic Delegation Process. It will increase employee engagement. This ability to delegate not only makes your job easier, but it will ultimately add dollars to the company's bottom line. Here's why:

> At the heart of employee engagement is empowering your employees every day to think for themselves. Socratic Delegation jump-starts this process.

- As empowerment increases, so will employee engagement.
- Employees will come up with solutions and make fewer mistakes.
- Overall productivity (and profitability) will increase.

"People who enjoy meetings should not be in charge of anything."

- Thomas Sowell

CHAPTER 2: HOW SOCRATIC DELEGATION BUILDS INFLUENCE OVER RESULTS

What is influence and why is it critical to you as a leader who wants to master delegation?

Definition of Influence

influence, noun

1. The capacity to have an effect on the **character or behavior** of someone or something, or the effect itself is greater than a person or thing with such a capacity. (*Collaborative Leader*)

2. The power arising out of **status,** contracts, or wealth. (*Command-and-Control Boss*)

Influence, verb (used with object), **influenced, influencing**

1. To exercise influence on; affect; sway:

   To influence a person

2. To move or impel (a person) to some action

   Outside factors influenced her to resign

Knowledge = Influence

The sheer volume of information people deal with is at a premium and, because things move so fast, it is more important than ever for companies to hear from employees of all levels.

In many organizations, the information flow is still generally top-down. That is, information and instructions come from the executives downward through layers of managers. Flipping this to bottom-up requires leaders to employ Socratic Delegation and ask significantly more questions than is common. This creates an environment in which leadership does more listening than talking.

You'll be pleasantly surprised (and sometimes amazed) at what you learn from your team when you stop talking so much. As the old saying goes, there's a reason people were born with one mouth and two ears.

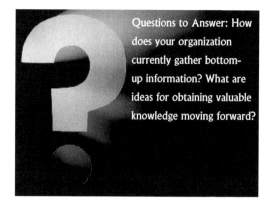

Questions to Answer: How does your organization currently gather bottom-up information? What are ideas for obtaining valuable knowledge moving forward?

Do you think of influence as the ability to impact circumstances? When you have influence, people respect you and want to please you, so BINGO! Influence does allow you to have more impact.

To increase your influence, keep in mind that you get what you expect. So when you attempt to delegate to others, if you do so with the mindset that you need to hold their hands or "fix" them, you'll get more evidence of their being broken and unable to meet the requirements you want.

"The key to successful leadership is influence, not authority."

— Kenneth Blanchard, best-selling author, *The One Minute Manager*

Give the Gift of Positive Expectation

As a leader, give others (and yourself!) the gift of positive expectation; it's key to having a work culture that thoroughly engages people. It also works wonders with those Millennials who already have confidence in their abilities and want you to recognize those abilities.

It starts when you wake up

• Do you wake up with a groan or a smile? Are you happy to be alive or is the jury still out? When my positive friend William wakes up, he tells me he raises both hands toward the ceiling and waves them around. "If I don't feel a coffin lid, I get out of bed, happy to have another day."

• As you're getting ready for work, are

your thoughts centered on expectations of a good day at work? Or are you already steeling yourself for problems?

The universal principle called Law of Attraction dictates that you get more of what you focus on. Shorthand for Law of Attraction is:

- If you expect negative experiences, that's what you get.
- When you expect positive experiences, life gets really good really fast—EVEN YOUR WORK LIFE.

Your Expectations Affect Productivity

You have a great opportunity each day to influence your company's culture by giving coworkers and those who report to you the gift of positive expectation. Expect people to do good work. Encourage them by catching them doing something right and let them know you noticed.

Practice this on yourself as well. Stop waiting for others to notice the great things you do. Keep your own file and encourage team members to do this as well—for themselves, not for you! Write *yourself* up for good performance.

Because you get more of what you focus on, tracking all the things you do well can result in your getting even better at your job and being even more productive. This is the same impact you can have when you focus on the good performance of others.

When you consider that negative expectations can be communicated without even saying a word, you realize the importance of shifting your opinion of those team members from whom you expect poor performance. Think about the impact on you when you become aware that someone whose opinion matters doesn't have faith in you. It's the same when you don't have faith in your team.

Point to Ponder #1: Psychologists say it takes seven positive statements to offset a negative one.

Perhaps your way of coping is to use others' negative expectations of you as fuel to try even harder. "I'll prove them wrong," you declare. Because this works for you, naturally you think having negative expectations of others will also motivate them. It might, but more likely they'll try so hard to avoid making mistakes, they'll only make more OR they will disengage, thinking, "If my boss doesn't believe in me, why bother?"

It's significantly more motivating to strive to live up to positive expectations than negative ones. When you have faith in others, they usually work hard because they don't want to let you down

And by the way, your expectations must be genuine. Employees can somehow tell when you're saying one thing ("I believe in you") while thinking another ("I doubt you can do it").

> "Your brain, at positive, performs significantly better than it does at negative, neutral or stressed."
>
> - TED Talk by Shawn Achor, author, *The Happiness Advantage*

When you have positive expectations of others, you go out of your way to notice things that support your faith in them. Conversely, when you have negative expectations, you notice things that support that negative belief. So, if you want to be "right" about something, why not lean toward the positive and use this belief to increase productivity?

Point to Ponder #2:
Human beings would rather be right than happy.

The Socratic Delegation Process is a substantive resource for changing your negative expectations of others. By systematically drawing out the implementation plans of your team, you will, over time, begin to see their capabilities and value.

Start practicing giving the gift of positive expectations. I'm not saying you won't be let down from time to time; you will. However, when you expect the best from others and watch for it, you'll be pleasantly surprised by how often they rise to meet your expectations. Employee engagement and productivity will increase; so will your influence and their morale.

If you have a team member who has a history of failure, Socratic Delegation could be the approach that turns him/her around. Try it for three months and gauge your results. If it doesn't make a difference, it may be time to find a replacement.

Consider this: If you were given the choice between being fully involved or bored to distraction, which would you choose? It's

> Start with the premise that everyone wants to be engaged!

the same answer for everyone, but many people don't know how to do this for themselves. That's where a collaborative approach to leadership comes in. Be sure to use Socratic Delegation to influence your team's involvement at a deeper level.

Beware of Influence Killers

Respected management consultant and author Margaret J. Wheatley specializes in organizational development. In the *Journal for Strategic Performance Measurement,* she wrote, *"You give someone clear instructions, written or verbal, and they always change it in some way, even just a little. They tweak it, reinterpret it, ignore parts of it, and add their own coloration or emphasis."*

How NOT to Delegate: Two Ways
What are the top ways to decrease your influence?

- Give unsolicited advice
- Give orders (command-and-control)

Wheatley described the three most common actions people take when given instructions; they

1. Ignore them
2. Change them
3. Criticize them

Notice that "following them to the letter" is not on the list. Most people, including your staff, do one of the three with your good ideas. Given that, why are you bothering to offer them? After all, as noted earlier,

NO ONE'S LISTENING!

". . . receiving orders provides no challenge to creativity, no summons to participation, no buy-in, and no honoring of people's intellectual talents."

— R. Brian Stanfield

If you doubt this truth, try this experiment. The next time you tell someone how to do something, pay close attention to that person's face. S/he may be looking right at you but not listening. Better still, follow up to see whether your idea was implemented. You will likely find that person did one of the three things Wheatley identified: ignore, change, or criticize

Reasons They Don't Follow Your Instructions to the Letter

Let's discuss, one-by-one, the reasons behind Wheatley's three identified responses in organizations today.

1. Why they *IGNORE* your instructions.

This is the answer to: "I work hard to give good directions, so why aren't they carried out correctly?'"

It's not that people ignore your instructions per se. More accurately, they don't even hear your instructions due to competing distractions. We are all swimming in NOISE. Sometimes, people hear what you are asking for but filter it through their experience and decide they know better. Or they miss important distinctions because what you asked for seems *similar* to a past task or project they did even though you know it's not the same. Other times, they're completely focused on their own good ideas for how they can accomplish what you've asked.

This happens even when you write down instructions! There are people who refer to manuals and others who do not. The more confidence your team members have in their abilities, the less likely they are to refer to your well-thought-out, detailed instructions, written or not. Some may even find them insulting. To see this more clearly, take a few minutes to identify a time when your instructions weren't carried out as given. What was your role in It?

> People ignore your ideas because they didn't really hear them in the first place!

2. Why they *CHANGE* your instructions.

Contrary to what you think, most people don't change your instructions out of rebellion (although sometimes that's true). Your instructions usually get adapted because they think they know a better way, especially when they consider this to be their area of expertise.

If you're a CEO and one of your customers tells you how to deliver something related to your product or service that you know won't work, aren't you obligated to push back? After all, your expertise and experience is the reason he bought from you in the first place. Of course, you'll take into consideration what he tells you. But in the end, because you are certain of your expertise, you're likely to get his buy-in on your method of delivery. You would do this because you feel confident the outcome will meet or exceed the customer's expectations, and doing it his way will not.

Likewise, the team members to whom you delegate know how to deliver the end product you request. After all, they were hired and trained to develop the expertise to do their particular jobs. Even though you supervise them, they should still know best how to produce results in their areas of responsibility but may be afraid to push back. When you tell them how to do their jobs, they are likely to adapt your instructions so they can produce the results they think you want in the way they know works best. Socratic Delegation gives you the means to find that out *before* action is taken.

3. Why they *CRITICIZE* your instructions.

Whenever you tell employees how to do a job they're considered knowledgeable about, your instructions are likely to be criticized. They'd say to their co-workers something like *"You won't believe how the boss wants me to do this. If I did it that way, it would take me twice as long. I'd like to see him do this job for a week—that would open his eyes to what we do around here!"*

People who criticize instructions may also have other deep-seated complaints such as these:

1. On rare occasions when they've been given feedback on their work, it's most often negative.
2. They don't think their boss knows or appreciates what they do.
3. They believe no one listens to them and/or they aren't treated with respect.

Some criticizers have been in their role for years and have developed a deep expertise. When that expertise is usurped by the instructions of an immediate supervisor (who may or may not have ever performed that task or job), they're understandably upset. That upset is commonly expressed in criticism of the boss, whether it's warranted or not

Getting the Results You Want

So how do you get the results you want? The answer to that question has these three components:

- Stop trying to control everything.
- Let your team support you.
- Connect with your team members' enthusiasm and expertise

Stop Trying to Control Everything

Have you ever noticed that the most powerful lessons you've learned were painful? I don't know about you, but some lessons I've had to learn repeatedly. Letting go of control is one.

You don't tell waiters how to serve you (at least I hope you don't!). You don't tell the workers who pick up your trash how to do it. You're happy to let the power company deliver your electricity without instructions from you.

We tend to allow others to support us when we know they can do it without our help. Start realizing that your team CAN do it without you. In fact, they'd probably do it a lot better without all your "help."

I invite you to begin looking at the world through a different set of eyes. Observe all the ways you already allow others to support you (cable company, internet providers, etc.) so you understand

> The mark of truly great leaders is that no one notices when they're not around. They have empowered their teams so well, they know what to do without the leaders' constant presence.

you are capable of allowing it. In fact, you do it every day. Wouldn't it be great if you could rely on your team in just the same way? You can! But it takes a collaborative leadership approach.

You don't expect Netflix to read your mind and know what you mean when you say, "I'd like to watch a movie." You need to give them more data so they can deliver the movies you want. So it is with your team. The more clarity you provide about the results you seek, the more they can deliver what you want without you telling them how to do it.

Place the same trust you have for vendors on your team. Then watch as more support comes your way!

Let Your Team Support You

Does this scenario seem familiar? You ask people to do something and, as they're doing it, you're micro-managing the process. This incident demonstrated it beautifully: I had asked my assistant to find a rental car. While he was on the phone, I was interrupting his conversation to feed him information. Y-U-C-K!

What is this need for control all about? It's too easy to say, "Well, it's a matter of trust. You don't trust others to do it correctly." That's often true but not in this case. I did trust him to do it right. But there's something deeper at work here.

In analyzing my behavior, I had to consider how often I do this. Not a pretty answer. Over the years, my track record has improved, but I still do it. Pondering my need for control, I realize the reason for any improvement has been the result of an increase in my self-esteem.

What's the connection? If you have low self-esteem, chances are you feel undeserving of assistance or support from others. Leaders who have reputations for being controlling may actually feel the least deserving. They assign tasks but then feel guilty about asking others to do more work. So they jump in and try to "help."

This is exactly what I was doing with my assistant—trying to make it easier for him. But recipients of this "help" don't see it that way; they view your attempts as a lack of trust. In the worst-case scenario, they interpret this behavior as meaning you actually regard them as incapable of doing what you've asked.

Think about your own behavior. When you're uncomfortable about asking others to do something, do you delegate and then assuage your guilt over making more work for them by trying to "help"? Control, then, is often a desire to make things easier for others so any guilt is appeased. I witness this in my work with front-line supervisors all the way up to the C-Suite. I continually run into kind-hearted individuals willing to drive themselves by working incredibly long hours but reluctant to assign tasks to others even when these tasks are part of their jobs!

Or have you adopted the admirable attitude that "the buck stops here" for the work your team does, fearing mistakes will reflect poorly on you? Since you always get more of what you focus on, when considering your behavior, ask, "Do my actions match up with what I want to receive?"

If you're uncomfortable with others doing for you (even if you're not conscious of it), or fear they won't do it right, you'll find reasons to do it yourself. How many times have you declared, "It's quicker and easier to do it myself"? And if we do it ourselves, we don't feel guilty about bothering others nor are we concerned it will be done correctly.

Our focus then becomes "No one can do this as well or as quickly as I can." Since you get more of what you focus on, guess what? You're right! No one can do it as well as you! If you have the time to do everything yourself, that's no problem. But what if you're the boss and you've hired people to perform these tasks? Not only are you doing your own work, you're also doing the work of others and complaining about it as if you have nothing to do with it!

The result? You get to feel righteous and you'll be alone at work for hours after your team members have gone home.

If you want to become less controlling and more influential, start by asking yourself if you feel uncomfortable having others do work for you and why. The most controlling people I know get pleasure from doing for others and yet, ironically, they deprive others of the same pleasure by their own inability to accept support.

If you want to build your influence so your team can be more supportive, start by being supportable. Understand that most people are happy to do what you ask—but NOT if you breathe down their necks while they're doing it

Look for Ways to Connect

Influence has everything to do with connection. "Do you and I connect? Do I enjoy our connection? Am I willing to be forthcoming with you?"

Having influence over another requires that people "let you in" at some level. The more they allow you "in," the more influence you're likely to have, either positive or negative. Don't mistake being allowed "in" as always having a positive impact. Sometimes the people you can't get out of your thoughts provide negative influences.

Do you remember your parents telling you one of your friends was a bad influence? You probably disagreed because you felt connected to this person; you had let him/her "in." If you're honest, you admit that his/her influence seemed thrilling to you.

> To delegate without having your instructions ignored, changed, or criticized, be willing to give up the delusion that you can control and know everything!

Or maybe some teachers who pointed out your shortcomings had a negative influence on you. Maybe you were continually in trouble for not doing things their way and their negativity included shaming in the classroom. Yet for shaming to work, you have to let that person "in," allowing him/her to influence you.

Influence is powerful and not to be taken lightly. If you have influence with someone, make sure you use it for good. Refuse to be a bad influence in any sense of the word.

Ways to connect with your team

Experiment with these ways of leading to connect and see what results emerge:

- **MBWA.** Manage by walking around. Do your team members have to do a perimeter search to find you? Are you always in your office or in meetings? Spend 10 minutes a day walking around and saying hello. You may be pleasantly surprised what a difference this makes in helping everyone feel connected. If you have distance workers, the equivalent to MBWA would be MBIM – management by instant messaging. Say hello at the beginning of the day to your distant workers; you'll both feel more connected and they'll be more comfortable reaching out to you on issues.

- **Say thank you.** An operations manager I once coached told me the owner of the business, whenever he was on site, stood by the time clock at the end of each day and personally thanked the workers as they clocked out. What is your version of this nicety?

- **Use performance review meetings to connect.** If you're only discussing staff performance annually, I guarantee your team feels disengaged. Have regular meetings with each team member to discuss how that person is performing against goals set. At a minimum, these meetings should be monthly, but weekly would be better. Most Millennials prefer daily feedback (I know! I know—don't shoot the messenger!). Meetings don't have to be lengthy. Set a limit to how many minutes you'll spend with each team member, pad it by five minutes, and then stick to that amount of time.

- **Fully utilize the tools you have.** If your company uses any sort of assessment tool (for example, DISC, Myers Briggs, Harrison Innerview, True Colors), use the information about each of your team members to assess how to best connect with him/her. If you don't use an assessment tool, research how using one could strengthen your influence.

- **Hold monthly or quarterly gatherings.** They can be lunch, morning coffee breaks, or TGIM (Thank God It's Monday) events.

- **Use (appropriate) humor.** A study of Canadian financial institutions found that teams with managers who used humor to connect with them significantly outperformed teams whose managers were always serious. If this works at buttoned-up financial institutions, imagine how well it would work with your team!

- **Celebrate milestones.** Examples are employment anniversaries, birthdays, and project launches and/or completions. What's most important when you do this? That YOU show up for these events and don't deem them as being only for the employees; this can be seen as condescending. And make note: Don't only think of hosting a party. Sending a personal note or card would also have a big impact.

- **Look for things to appreciate about your team members.** Remember, you get more of what you focus on. Even if you don't share all your observations, they can tell when you are appreciating them. It will show up in your demeanor—and go a long way toward building connections.

- **Write them up when they do well.** A city supervisor, a self-described "blue collar guy," participated in one of my collaborative leadership programs. He got frustrated with my suggestion that he formally write people up not only for mistakes they make but for things they do well. He said, "You mean I have to acknowledge them for just doing their jobs?" Rather than talk him into doing this, I asked him this question: "Dave, if each of your team came in every day and just did their jobs, would your life be a whole lot easier?" His response was, "It sure would!" I leaned back and said, "THAT'S why you want to acknowledge them for just doing their jobs. It's important they know someone sees their good work and appreciates it. The more you notice them doing the work they were hired to do, the more of it they'll do!" (I recently checked in with Dave and, with a sheepish grin, he told me this approach was working beautifully.)

It's Okay to Use Command-and-Control Sometimes

Just tell your team that you're doing it! But only use command-and-control to influence your people when it's appropriate. For example:

- **When safety is an issue.** If your house is on fire, you certainly don't want the fire chief asking her team for input on how to put it out. She must issue orders fast! In military-style organizations, command-and-control is necessary when soldiers are on any kind of duty involving danger. Although they aren't strictly military-style organizations, hospitals also need to revert to command-and-control in emergency situations. This is most evident in the ER or when a Code Blue emergency occurs in a patient's room.

- **When a deadline looms and action has to happen fast.** Sometimes you don't have time for input; you simply need to move. When that happens, it's best to say to your team, "Okay, we are in crisis mode. I'm taking off my collaborative hat and putting on my command-and-control hat. I need you to carry out my instructions quickly."

In both cases, when you clarify why you're switching gears, you'll avoid hard feelings and gain cooperation.

Unless command-and-control is necessary, using the Socratic Delegation Process gets the person to whom you're delegating quickly engaged. So employ it at the beginning of any new initiative and watch how quickly your team becomes involved. Of course, if your team has been accustomed to

Insider Tip:
Hold onto your hat! Once they get comfortable with Socratic Delegation, your team members will love you for seeking their input.

you simply telling them what to do and how to do it, the initial shock of your new delegation approach might be significant. Let them know what you're doing and why so they can be part of shifting the culture instead of feeling suspicious about what the heck is going on.

Conclusion ->

Having influence over results is not a process you put into place and then you're done. It requires daily evaluation of the current status to determine what tools to employ to get the results you want. Socratic Delegation is a good place to start. Having said that, sometimes command-and-control is the only way to meet a deadline. At other times, you'll need to shift your expectations, and often you'll be required to use tools

> The greatest leader is not necessarily the one who does the greatest things. He is the one that gets the people to do the greatest things. — Ronald Reagan, 40th President of the United States

listed in the section "Ways to connect with your team" such as MBWA, humor, or group meetings. Being an influential leader demands continual course correction as you lead your team to achieving success.

i. Margaret J. Wheatley & Keliner-Rogers, Myron, "Bringing Life to Organizational Change," *Journal for Strategic Performance Measurement*, April/May 1998.
ii. Dr. Bruce J. Avolio, Dr. Jane M. Howell, and Dr. John J. Sosik. "A Funny Thing Happened on the Way to the Bottom Line." Presented at the national meeting of the Society of Industrial and Organizational Psychology in San Diego, 1996.

"The key to being a good manager is keeping the people who hate me away from those who are still undecided."

- Casey Stengel

CHAPTER 3: USING SOCRATIC DELEGATION TO GAIN INFLUENCE WITH YOUR TEAM

Because you are in charge of your team, department, division, or company, do you also believe you're the designated problem-solver? If yes, you pay a price for this. When you're the "answer person," life quickly gets tiresome.

Camille, a coaching client, is director of a large public agency. She hired me to work with her on developing her staff into problem-solvers. She couldn't leave the office for 10 minutes without her cell phone ringing, a staff member on the line seeking her input on a situation and what to do. You can imagine what a chore it was for her to try and take a vacation!

It didn't take long to identify the source of the problem: Camille. She had inadvertently trained her staff to be dependent. Every time a team member suggested a solution or approach, she'd say, "I can tell you put a lot of thought into that and I appreciate it very much. But I think the best approach would be _____." Then she'd lay out her own plan.

When I pointed this out to Camille, she protested, "I don't do it to disempower them. It's just that I've been doing this for a long time. If they do it my way, it will save a lot of time and trouble."

So I gently asked, "And how did you learn it?" The answer, of course, was through trial-and-error—the very process she was eliminating from her team's learning process.

Does this dependency cycle sound uncomfortably familiar? Instead of demonstrating their own initiative, taking personal responsibility, and maximizing their own potential, employees "delegate up." In effect, they give problems they should solve themselves to the managers above them in the organization.

> Every single interaction with a team member is an opportunity for that person's growth and your freedom.

Giving Up Control to Gain Influence

How can you give up being the only problem-solver and, at the same time, gain more influence over your team and their results without actually doing the work yourself? Consider using these approaches:

1. Give up control over how team members achieve results
2. Allow them to take ownership
3. Have more collaborative conversations
4. Allow team members time to think
5. Know where to spend your time and leadership focus

Let's explore these one by one.

1. Give Up Control over How Team Members Achieve Results

Do you find yourself wondering why there aren't more self-sufficient people? Consider whether you're squelching any spark of initiative by countermanding every approach your employees come up with (as Camille did). You may be teaching your people to wait for you to solve their problems because, well, you always do.

As with Camille, assistance is usually offered out of compassion and a desire to be helpful. You see the discomfort of the other person struggling to find solutions and, ever ready to assist, you jump in. But the help you provide doesn't allow room for the all-important learning that comes from employees figuring out solutions on their own.

Let's be frank. Sometimes it's not compassion at all; our egos get in the way. I often hear, "It's just easier to do it myself. I already know how and I don't have time for someone else to figure it out." This comes from the same martyrs who complain, "I have to do everything around here." You can continue to do that but understand that your staff will be tethered to you in a way that's unpleasant for all of you. More than that, it keeps them stagnant when both you and the organization need them to grow.

Each of us desires control over our own destinies. If you ever wonder why some homeless people are adamant about staying on the streets versus accepting shelter when it's offered, it's often because they are determined to control their own day-to-day existence.

> "Great leaders focus on outcomes versus style."
>
> — Marcus Buckingham, Donald O. Clifton, *Now Discover Your Strengths*

Your team members are no different! ("Wait," you're thinking, "Did Silver just compare my team to the homeless?") They, too, want control over how they approach the various elements required to do their jobs.

A former boss of mine who'd been schooled in England once stood over my shoulder and expressed dismay at the way I was adding up a column of figures. In elementary school, I was taught a very specific way to do this. As it turns out, so was he, and our two methods were very different. And yet, when he showed me how he added the same column of figures, his answer matched mine! Of course, if our teachers had ever met, both would have insisted their way was the only way to do it correctly.

Today we understand that everyone's brain processes differently, Observe any elementary math class, and you'll see the kids are allowed to add columns of figures any way they want as long as they arrive at the correct answer. Similarly, team members should be allowed to achieve results in their own style. They won't approach every task or project the way you might because they don't all think the same as you do. This needn't be a problem as long as the result is the one you want!

Instead of giving instructions and suggestions, use Socratic Delegation to empower people by asking them questions about how to approach tasks and projects. Your team members want control over their destinies at work. If you continually tell them how to do things, you rob them of that experience. Maybe they can't control what is required of them, but certainly they deserve to have some influence over how they perform assignments.

2. Allow Them to Take Ownership

Among the many things that keep people from assuming ownership of their work is having no say in how to do what you're asking of them. In effect, Socratic Delegation allows them to "own" each task or project specifically because of their input into how to do them. If you bemoan the fact that others won't take responsibility for their work and then insist they do it your way, the quickest way to change that dynamic is by using Socratic Delegation.

If the person to whom you are delegating reveals that s/he plans to use a method that doesn't take into consideration pertinent facts or goes against company policy, then coaching from you is in order. However, if the only reason you want to correct this person's approach is because you have a better idea, keep it to yourself. How will she learn if you do all the thinking? And how can she experience self-worth by simply carrying out your solutions? Resist the temptation to sacrifice someone else's self-worth at the altar of your ego. And what if (this is a scary thought, I know) that person's idea for how to do it turns out to be better than yours?

Hone the Socratic Delegation process to fit your team culture. Because there are as many cultures as there are people reading this book, I can't tell you precisely how to apply it in your organization.

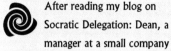 After reading my blog on Socratic Delegation: Dean, a manager at a small company wrote me this note: "Awesome! What a timely reminder for me not to over-manage. I'm constantly railing about how people learn by doing—not by being told or reading. Yet I continue to leap into problems because my ego knows how to fix them. I can't teach empowerment to people I treat like marionettes."

However, a good first step would be to let your team know you're planning to try it. Give them each a copy of the process and gather their input on how to best employ it. (You can download a copy of Socratic Delegation Step-by-Step at my website www.SilverSpeaks.com)

They may attempt to talk you out of it, telling you it's unnecessary or even insulting. But be firm. Often they are reacting out of fear or a natural resistance to change. Give it a three- to six-month trial and gauge the results. If productivity increases, mistakes decrease, and "ownership" occurs, you're on the right path.

In survey after survey when employees are asked what they want, money is never the top issue. High on the list of answers is being involved and valued by their organizations. Gathering their input on how to do things makes employees feel valued. This concept is sometimes difficult for managers to accept. It's easier to think employees aren't performing because the company can't or won't pay them enough. This thinking lets the manager off the hook. Knowing instead that you can provide a more satisfying culture for your employees requires effort on your part. However, I promise that, not only will it be more satisfying for the whole team, but you won't have to work nearly as hard! I've seen it time and time again.

Using Socratic Delegation provides the means for more team involvement, which brings us to the third way to gain more influence over your team: collaborative conversations.

3. Have More Collaborative Conversations

Most of what passes today for conversation consists of two people waiting their turns to talk. While one person is speaking, the other is busy formulating a comeback. So much gets missed that way.

 When you use dialogue instead of monologue to influence others, you're having a collaborative conversation.

Have you ever asked one of your employees, "Do you understand?" and heard an affirmative answer? What do you think they're likely to say? "Oh, I'm sorry, boss. While you were talking, I was in my head planning my next vacation." Of COURSE, employees will say they understand. When they walk away from the conversation, they are relying on one of two things: (1) figuring it out once they start the work, or (2) asking a co-worker to show them.

Your ability to have collaborative conversations is the linchpin for influence and the perfect replacement for command-and-control. In a command-and-control exchange, the supervisor does 80-90% of the talking. S/he gives instructions while the person mostly listens and (if you're lucky) asks clarifying questions. Often, you'll hear the occasional, "Yes," or "I understand."

By contrast, a collaborative conversation occurs when you and your team dialogue about how to approach a task or a project. To be most effective, you do 20% of the talking by providing context or asking questions, and the person being delegated to does 80% of the talking by filling you in on plans for producing the result you've asked for.

Your mission, should you choose to accept, is to create a culture of collaboration. That in turn establishes an environment in which your employees are involved, invested, interested, engaged, and even excited from time to time. The Socratic Delegation process stimulates collaborative conversations.

 The more your team members believe they have a say in how they perform their jobs, the more influence you will have with them

Remember this adage: "People don't leave jobs; they leave bosses." The truth is never quite that simple; a myriad of reasons exist to influence individuals to leave their jobs. It is undeniable, however, that a person's boss has a significant impact on his/her job satisfaction. When the supervisor doesn't know how to have collaborative conversations and doesn't delegate well, employees get discouraged and disengaged, and they often disembark.

4. Allow Team Members Time to Think

Time to think is an important component of collaborative conversations. For some members of your team, having an effective dialogue means letting them know a day in advance what you want to discuss. This allows them time to formulate their ideas. If that's not possible, make sure not to push for quick answers during the conversation. Again, give them time to consider what you're asking. When you do, you'll come to a solution or plan that both of you have bought into. If they feel pushed, they'll agree to what you want but won't take ownership.

The best leaders have not only learned how to ask good questions but also how to listen without bias or expectation. When you insist on the other person answering "your way," then you may as well answer the questions yourself. On the other hand, if you listen with curiosity about what s/he might say, then you're open to possibilities beyond your own

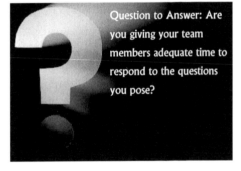

Question to Answer: Are you giving your team members adequate time to respond to the questions you pose?

knowledge. That's when you see the value of your employees—when you allow them to contribute new information and new perspectives.

5. Know Where to Spend Your Time and Leadership Focus

If Socratic Delegation is a new approach for you, it will take time for it to work. After three months of consistent and even-handed application, you should be able to identify team members' levels of performance including their abilities to come up with strategies, take ownership, be accountable, and produce results. At that point, you'll want to apply the 80/20 Rule of Good Leadership.

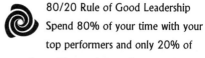

80/20 Rule of Good Leadership
Spend 80% of your time with your top performers and only 20% of your time with your low performers.

Spending most of your time with top performers could be considered management heresy, but think about it. If you give 80% of your time to your low performers trying to shore them up, you may (if you're lucky) get a 2-5% increase in productivity. If instead you spend 80% of your time with your top performers, you'll see an increase of 10-20% or more. Where is your time best invested?

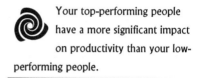

Your top-performing people have a more significant impact on productivity than your low-performing people.

To retain your top talent requires you to demonstrate to your whole team that performance counts. To emphasize this, devote 80% of your leadership time to your top performers and only 20% to those who aren't making the grade. That's counter-intuitive, isn't it? Yet how many wasted hours do leaders spend trying to save the often unsalvageable, low-level performers?

You cannot teach people something they don't want to learn.

Your low-level performers have undoubtedly been given many opportunities to improve. Maybe you have mentored them, used Socratic Delegation, sent them to classes, and/or put them on performance improvement plans—all to no avail. Although you've given them the best opportunity to deliver the outcomes your organization pays them for, they're taking up the bulk of your attention at the expense of time spent with your top performers. It's a recipe for trouble.

When you withdraw the majority of your attention from your low performers, one of three things will happen. They will:

1. Step up to the plate

2. Continue as they were, which leaves you no worse off, or

3. Leave. You can wish them well and hire a more suitable replacement.

The 80/20 Rule of Leadership also leverages your focus. Since you get more of what you focus on, as you work with your top performers your attention and theirs will be on increasing performance and fulfilling the organization's mission. Since both you and they already have great faith in their ability to do that, productivity will spiral upwards more quickly than you dared hope.

Your Top Talent Could Walk!

Your top performers don't need your attention to do their jobs; you can depend on them under most circumstances. However, if you continually demonstrate the way to get attention in your organization is to perform at a low level, your top talent might walk out the door. That's a high risk in today's intense competition for talent!

Recruiters are calling your top performers. You cannot possibly compete against the allure of their promises unless your employees feel appreciated for the talent, skill, and knowledge they bring to their work every day.

Conclusion ->

The most successful leaders build and sustain influence with their team by allowing as much control as possible over how they achieve objectives and then holding them accountable.

Try Socratic Delegation! You're likely to see some team members wake up to the opportunity to apply their own ideas. You'll see others who've been "checked out" stepping up in a new way, and Millennials will wonder what took you so long to ask for their input. Give your low performers every opportunity, but if they

> "Average leaders raise the bar on themselves, good leaders raise the bar for others, great leaders inspire others to raise their own bar." – Orrin Woodward, Chairman, Board of Life Leadership, New York Times bestselling author, *And Justice for All: The Quest for Concord*

repeatedly decline your invitations to improve, then employ the 80/20 rule.

Remember, give the majority of your time and focus to your top performers who have shown they want to work toward achieving the intended results. All of this will free you from being "the answer person" for everything. Then you and your team will have more collaborative conversations, which naturally leads to more employee engagement.

CHAPTER 4: DEVELOP MOTIVATED TEAM MEMBERS WHO THINK FOR THEMSELVES

No matter where you fall in the leadership spectrum—owner, executive, manager, supervisor, project manager, or team lead—you are a teacher. As such, you know that self-esteem is achieved in large part through learning. In a work situation, we call it talent development or mentoring. Remember Socrates? His Socratic Method used questions as a way to teach. And Socratic Delegation accomplishes the same.

Does this dependency cycle sound uncomfortably familiar? Instead of demonstrating their own initiative, taking personal responsibility, and maximizing their own potential, employees "delegate up." In effect, they give problems they should solve themselves to the managers above them in the organization.

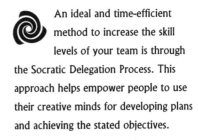 An ideal and time-efficient method to increase the skill levels of your team is through the Socratic Delegation Process. This approach helps empower people to use their creative minds for developing plans and achieving the stated objectives.

Don't Tell—Teach!

Developing motivation in others happens most effectively through teaching, not telling them how to do it. Decades of empirical data support the thesis: asking good questions promotes successful performance and builds cultures focused on learning. By comparison, being told what to do and how to do it implies incompetence and/or inability. This can result in a culture of low productivity.

Why We Tell Instead of Teach

Here are three common excuses people use to "tell" versus "teach" at work:

1. "It's faster."
2. "I'm the boss; I have more experience."
3. "Employees prefer it."

Let's take them one by one.

#1. "It's faster." I won't argue the validity of this; it's usually true. In case of an emergency or an important, impending deadline, this is an appropriate way to get things done, fast! In other circumstances, however, it's short-term thinking and, as a leader, you're paid to take a long-term view. When you insist on performing tasks that members of your team are paid for, you do yourself, your organization, and each team member a big disservice in these ways:

- You work harder than you need to. If you're still at work when your employees are long gone, think about why you're doing their work for them.
- While you're doing that person's job, you're not doing the job you're paid to do, which costs the organization.
- Your team member misses an opportunity to learn something and grow.

#2. "I'm the boss; I have more experience." This one I am challenging. Even if you do have more experience, you have team members who are paid to be responsible for specific areas. The ideal is for them to bypass your experience and knowledge. If you know more about the individual components of your division than those directly responsible for them, then you're doing a poor job of teaching and delegating.

Why don't you want that to be true? When it's time for a promotion, if your department still needs you to function day-to-day, you'll likely be overlooked because it would cause too much disruption in your department—and ultimately in the organization. And just like Camille in Chapter 3, you can kiss uninterrupted vacations goodbye. Guaranteed, you'll get calls and emails. If you are a business owner, this dependency

 Being indispensable in your company, especially when it comes to getting the basic work done, is a trap—one that traps you, your employees, and your company.

makes your company less attractive to potential buyers. They won't buy your business if it can't run without you.

#3. Employees prefer teaching over telling. If I weren't sick of seeing the acronym LOL everywhere, I'd repeatedly stamp LOL (laughing out loud) all over this.

Okay, let me be nice. I'm certain some of your employees have said, "Just tell me how you want it done and I'll do it." They didn't start out wanting to be told what to do. It's just that slowly, over time, they have come to realize it's easier. They resign themselves to your lack of delegation skills. They surrender to doing it your way. They get tired of you either not soliciting their input or overriding it. Perhaps they have grown weary of negative feedback for outcomes that were never clearly outlined. And yes, some may have never been given the opportunity to think for themselves and simply don't know how, but they'd like to learn.

With new employees or team members who have been transferred to a new role, some training necessarily takes the form of telling them how to do things. However, once they've gotten the basics, it's important to switch to the Socratic Delegation process. It will help you assess their level of understanding. Remember, they're approaching this new role with a fresh pair of eyes, and they may have some questions or good ideas that will help to improve the process. These can easily surface when you use Socratic Delegation.

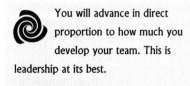 You will advance in direct proportion to how much you develop your team. This is leadership at its best.

Allow Employees to Make Mistakes

As a senior in high school, I worked evenings and weekends at a department store. My boss was Mr. Keenan, a man I thought was very worldly and incredibly smart. One day, I went to "confess" to Mr. Keenan that I'd made a mistake. (I was raised Catholic; confession is in my DNA.) I proceeded to tell him how stupid my mistake was and how I couldn't believe I'd done such a dumb thing. I babbled until he finally raised his hand in the universal signal for "Stop" and said, "Silver, I don't care if you make mistakes. That's how you learn, and it shows me you're trying. Just don't make the same mistake twice!"

I was flabbergasted. What? No punishment? No acts of contrition? Not even a single Hail Mary?!? This marked the first time anyone had ever given me permission to make mistakes. I thought Mr. Keenan was the wisest man in the

world. (Amazing since he was only 25 years old!) Young though he was, he knew what all good leaders know—that mistakes signal your team members are trying. He was smart enough to tell me the boundaries—"don't make the same mistake twice"—and deliver praise instead of shame.

As I write this, Samsung Corporation has launched a massive worldwide recall of several products. Insiders describe the culture of fear that has been bred there—one in which instructions given by supervisors cannot be questioned and mistakes aren't tolerated. It's a petri dish for producing flawed products.

In one instance, Samsung had to recall Galaxy Note7 cell phones because the battery inside could explode. In every airport I traveled through for months, travelers were told the Federal Aviation Administration has issued an edict banning possession of this model cell phone on airplanes. Agents and flight attendants made this announcement before each plane took off. Imagine what that did to the brand image!

It's likely true that Samsung produced products faster than its competitors because of its management style. But does the company produce good products? The proof, as my grandmother used to say, is in the pudding. And don't get too close to that pudding lest it explode.

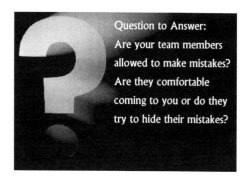

Question to Answer: Are your team members allowed to make mistakes? Are they comfortable coming to you or do they try to hide their mistakes?

The Thrill of Seeing the Spark Ignite!

Have you ever watched someone's face light up when s/he suddenly "gets" something that's been a struggle—when a key understanding clicks into place? Nothing is more exciting or fulfilling than igniting a spark in someone else. In the case of engagement, you won't always have the equivalent of a lighter at hand to create an instant flame. More often, it resembles the approach we learned in Scouting—patiently rub two sticks together until a spark catches the kindling. But how satisfying it is to see the first flame!

When you delegate using the time-worn command-and-control method, it does little to increase your knowledge of what team members are thinking or can do. Nor does it increase their ability to problem-solve or think for themselves. And it's a sure way to douse any spark that might be ready to ignite.

 No matter your level of management, your role as a leader is to produce results through people. This requires igniting sparks.

When, on the other hand, you apply Socratic Delegation, you can develop your knowledge of each team member's thought processes when it comes to working and achieving results. Understanding those thought processes is key to leading effectively and delegating to the appropriate employee.

Honor Their Expertise

Don't you love it when someone calls on you for your expertise—when they ask your opinion because they know you're the "go to person" on that topic? When your knowledge and experience get acknowledged, you're happy to step up to the plate and deliver.

If you've ever visited an elementary school classroom on Parents Day or Grandparents Day, remember how excited your child felt showing you everything? Eyes shining, s/he took you by the hand and dragged you all over to show you his/her world. "Here's my desk. These are my crayons. Here's my art project on the wall. This is my poetry essay. This is my best friend." We never get beyond the trill of this wonderful feeling because the child we were still lives within. We want people we love, admire, and respect to see what our world is like, including

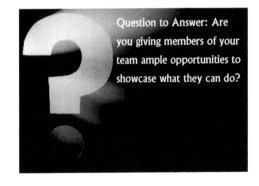

Question to Answer: Are you giving members of your team ample opportunities to showcase what they can do?

all we do and what we've accomplished.

Your employees are no different.

Your team is comprised of in-house consultants—experts at what they do. Are you tapping that expertise? Are you acknowledging their accomplishments? I don't mean in a formal performance review or in feedback mode. Rather, are you acknowledging their expertise by asking them to weigh in on tasks and projects related to their assigned areas?

A follow-up question would be: Do you bring in outside consultants without first looking in-house? If team members haven't even been asked about the improvements the consultant has been brought in to achieve, they will resist having external advisers around. On the other hand, if they do provide input and you still bring in a consultant, you'll have a smoother transition—especially if you personally introduce the consultant to your team while articulating the in-house expertise of each.

A Brilliant Example of Honoring Expertise

If it hasn't happened to you, you've read about it or it's happened to someone you know. People get stranded at a busy airport because their flight was cancelled. My client Shawn handled this in a unique way. His story provides a great example of how to influence others based on these principles:

- Think differently
- Let the experts share their expertise.
- Let others solve your problem.
- Use influence as a win/win.
- Know that people love to help

When Shawn, a seasoned business traveler, heard the cancellation announcement over the PA late in the evening, his stomach sank; he knew the chance of catching another flight was slim. Watching a familiar scene unfold in front of him, he saw angry passengers crowd the airline's customer service desk being exceedingly rude to the unfortunate agents behind it. The agents, who had nothing to do with the cancellation, were losing patience. Tempers were flaring.

Think differently. Shawn asked himself, "Who would know how to get me to my destination?" When the answer came to him, he grabbed his coat and briefcase and headed for a different customer service desk with agents present. Happily, their most recent flight had just left, and they had no customers waiting in line.

As he approached the agents' desk, Shawn glanced at the nametag of the agent who made eye contact with him and smiled at her. "Leticia, can I ask you something?" Smiling back, she said, "Of course." In a pleasant tone without placing blame, he laid out his dilemma: the flight cancellation, the fact that he needed to be in Detroit in the morning for an important business meeting, and so on. Then Shawn posed a savvy question, "If you were in my shoes, what would you do?"

Let the experts share their expertise. This businessman who'd been promoted to his company's C-Suite because of his strong leadership skills had learned long ago that people love opportunities to share their expertise. Sure enough, Leticia and the other agent Julio couldn't wait to give Shawn all their inside tips to solve his problem. By the time he left their counter, he had a ticket for a flight that would guarantee his arrival in Detroit long before his meeting started.

Let others solve your problem. Most of us don't like to receive unsolicited advice, but we're really happy when someone turns to us to help solve a problem. We love to solve problems, particularly other people's problems. So imagine actually being invited to do so. How thrilling! I can see you rubbing your hands in happy anticipation. So did those airline agents!

 When pondering the problems you need to solve at work, consider that your team members would love to be asked for their input!

Use influence as a win/win. The next time you have a thorny problem, ask, "Who on the team would know how to fix this?" and then ask this wonderful question posed by Shawn: *"If you were in my shoes, what would you do?"* The person you ask will be pleased you recognize his/her expertise, and you just may be presented with an innovative solution.

Know that people love to help. Our society places great value on lending a hand. In the aftermath of natural disasters, we witness heart-warming acts of support through stories in the news. Think about this: Many of the fairy tales read to us as children involve a kind of rescue scenario. In fact, we've cut our teeth on this concept. So when you ask people to help, you are giving them an opportunity to do something they enjoy—a win/win of the best kind.

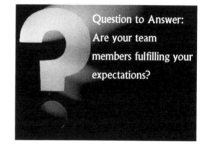

A Caveat

If someone provides a solution and you don't use it or you hesitate to do so, let him/her know. Why? Some people get offended if they think they've solved your problem and then discover you didn't take their advice. To avoid this, say something like, "I really appreciate your thoughts. I'll have to make the decision myself, but your input helps me think it through."

Focus on What You Want to See More Of

Your team members have the same desire as you—to use their expertise to advance tasks and projects. Before they can do that, though, they must understand your needs and expectations. As noted earlier in Give the Gift of Positive Expectations, this can be a double-edged sword. If you watch for the worst of someone, you often get it. If you look for the best, you get that instead.

I cannot emphasize enough how what you anticipate can make or break performance.

I'm not talking about fulfilling the objectives stated on their job descriptions or performance improvement plans. Rather, I'm talking about what you have internalized about each of them:

She's not leadership material and never will be.

I can always rely on him to deliver.

He's undependable.

Question to Answer: Are your team members fulfilling your expectations?

We often make assessments of people based on little empirical data. This is true whether the judgment is positive or negative. A negative impression can form and "stick" based on one mistake. Conversely, when a team member delivers quality on the first project you see, in your mind, s/he's terrific. Once you assess your team member that way, it's tough to see that person in any other light.

We often unconsciously fulfill what others focus on about us. Early in my childhood, my father and brothers teased me about being clumsy; they bandied about the term "klutz" a lot. But I swear the ONLY time I displayed this clumsiness was when they were around. Suddenly, I forgot how to walk without tripping over my feet and dropped things for no good reason. In my efforts to prove I wasn't clumsy, my total focus was on "klutz"—and that's the expectation I unconsciously fulfilled.

Articulated in this context, "You get more of what you focus on" becomes "you get more of what you expect."

What biases do you have about your team, and do you unconsciously find ways to be "right" about your expectations? If you have determined that someone is lazy, for example, your mind will accumulate a tremendous amount of data to prove your thesis. Because of this tendency, I developed a rule that goes a long way toward getting out of this trap. I call it The Court of Law Rule.

The Court of Law Rule

If you can't prove it in a court of law, it's a story you made up.

Can you prove people are lazy? You cannot. However, you can prove they don't show up for work on time, their assignments are consistently late, and their eyes are closed during meetings. But you can't prove they're lazy unless they say to you (preferably in front of a reliable witness), "I am lazy."

Persistent negative judgments often stop direct supervisors from developing employees to their fullest. Labeling them (even silently) as lazy, stupid, or a troublemaker creates a major obstacle to seeing and exploring their capabilities.

Another way to say it is this: "You get more of what you measure."

Clarify How Success is Measured

How is performance measured in your organization? It's completely unfair to your team when you're not clear about this. For example, if you ask them to improve their "teamwork," how will they know when that goal has been fulfilled? How will the kind of teamwork you desire be specifically measured? If the immediate supervisor can't answer that question, then employees are being set up for failure, and problems begin. And if the company as a whole is unclear about how they measure performance, then the problem is systemic.

On the flip side, employees can and should insist on knowing the specific measurements for their jobs. "How is my performance measured?" is a question every employee must be able to answer if s/he wants to succeed. And if you, their leader, don't have clarity about your role in the company, you're setting yourself up for failure.

As I write this, we're in the midst of the National Basketball Association (NBA) playoffs. As a result, I have been considering how measurement works in professional sports, all of which are businesses with multiple employees. All of those employees—the general manager, head coach, trainers, players, and more—understand they're being assessed based on their contributions toward making the organization profitable.

For players, this translates into all the stats you hear announcers discuss during the game. Some players rarely score but are credited with "assists" that cause someone else on the team to score. Others have the job of preventing the opposing team from scoring. The coach, of course, is measured by the team's win/loss record during the season. It should come as no surprise that the players who either score the most points or make the biggest contribution to the team's success end up making the most money. They've demonstrated their value to the team. No one in the NBA ever got a raise because of seniority or because they "worked hard."

Questions to Answer: What measurements do you have in place? Does each team member know how his/her performance is being measured?

If you want to gain more influence over your team's results fast, figure out what and how to measure performance—a critical component of good delegation.

Too many on your team measure themselves against whether or not they're working hard. If you went to a dentist who botched a filling, would you want to hear, "But I worked really hard to get it right!"? Unlikely. You'd be totally focused on the fact that you experienced unnecessary pain because of the dental work.

Ironically, if you and your team begin measuring performance against predetermined results instead of how hard they're working, you all may not have to work nearly as hard. Or maybe they'll discover they need to work even harder because they're not achieving the results. Remember, you attract more of what you measure. Make sure everyone is measuring results, not effort.

Definitions Matter

One of the easiest communication problems to solve when delegating revolves around our tendency to think that others understand what we mean when we use a term. Let's take "customer service," as an example.

If you tell your team to improve customer service, what does that mean? How is customer service being defined? If you have Millennials on your team, where might they have even experienced good customer service? They may be thinking "the Apple store" with its controlled chaos while you're thinking "Nordstrom's" with its classical piano playing in the background. Not only do different generations differ in their understanding of terms, individuals within each generation do, as well. So when you are delegating, find out whether their definitions of the terms you are using match.

Giving people edicts to improve something without telling them what it should look like is unfair and sets up a "no win" situation.

Always answer the unspoken question, "How will we measure success?" and make sure everyone is on the same page by defining terms.

No one gets rewarded for working hard if the results don't follow. Conversely, if the results can be produced without working hard, excellent! And PLEASE don't be the type of organization that immediately "rewards" good results with more work!

The Golden Phrase: "As Evidenced By" Years ago, a nurse manager told me the story that has always stuck with me: When I work with my employees on performance improvement, I make sure they understand exactly what is required. I cannot simply tell them to increase the quality of patient care; I must say, "Increase the quality of patient care as evidenced by an increase in positive patient survey scores and a reduction in the number of formal complaints."

Conclusion ->

If you want to develop motivated team members who can think for themselves, provide opportunities for them to do so. By exchanging a "telling" leadership approach with "teaching and mentoring" in the style of Socrates, you will develop your employees into independent problem-solvers who become experts in their areas of responsibility. Once they are experts, honor their expertise by calling on them to fully utilize it.

> "The best executive is the one who has sense enough to pick good men to do what he wants done and self-restraint to keep from meddling with them while they do it." — Theodore Roosevelt

Challenge your expectations. Can your assessments of your team be proven in a court of law? Are you stuck on old data? Importantly, clarify how success is measured. Another way to say, "You get more of what you focus on" is "You get more of what you measure."

What are you measuring and do your team members know?

CHAPTER 5: THE IMPORTANT ROLE OF MISSION IN DELEGATION

When sufficiently inspired, even marginal workers turn into valuable employees when they understand the "why" behind the work they do.

I have often marveled at the endless hours and thousands of dollars leaders spend crafting a Mission Statement that even the CEO can't recite from memory. Every leader in your organization should be able to recite the Mission Statement if woken up from a dead sleep and asked to do so. If not, your organization is in deep trouble.

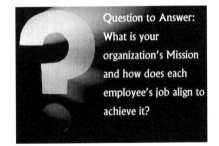

Question to Answer: What is your organization's Mission and how does each employee's job align to achieve it?

"Where the Hell are We Going?"

Imagine trying to coach a team to win a new game you've invented without telling the players the rules or what winning looks like. How would they know how to win!?

Does your team know where you're taking the organization? Are you sure? One way to find out is to ask, "What am I leading them toward? What's the destination?" If you don't know the answers right off the top of your head, think how confused your people must be!

One reason employee engagement is so low (barely 33% according to Gallup) is that workers are turned into lemmings, trained to follow the dictates of their immediate supervisor without question. They show up each day and do what they assume are priorities, yet they have no sense of whether they're moving closer to the team's goal or further away. Why?

It's either because they're not sure what the goal IS or they don't see how their work supports it.

Igniting Their Inspiration and Passion

 Just showing up and working isn't a big enough game for those on your team, and that's why they become disengaged.

Too many employees' primary aim is to get through the day without showing up on anyone's radar screen. They do enough of the job to stay out of trouble but leave their inspiration and passion at home. So how can you change this?

First, it's important that you take the appropriate action to:

1. **Identify and completely understand the goal/destination** to which you are leading your team.

2. **Clearly communicate your goal/destination to the team**, including

- How the goal supports the larger organization's current goals/destination.

- How it fits in with the overall Mission and Vision of the organization.

3. **Solicit your team's input for how to get to the goal/destination.**

4. **Become a walking, breathing scoreboard of measures.**

> "If you hire people just because they can do a job, they'll work for your money. But if you hire people who believe what you believe, they'll work for you with blood and sweat and tears."
>
> — Simon Sinek, author

Your team members reflect your level of engagement. If you're floundering, they will flounder. If you're clear about where you're taking them, they'll be clear. If you're engaged, they'll be engaged.

Please don't mistake engagement for working hard. In fact, when you are fully engaged in the work, it doesn't feel hard at all. When engaged, you continually seek ways to improve the end product, develop processes to achieve results faster and/or better, and grow your own skill set and knowledge base. Let's discuss each of these.

1. Identify and completely understand the team's goal/destination.

This might seem obvious and yet how often, when you try to articulate where you're going, does it becomes confusing? When you did the four activities noted above, did you discover that to be true? Or were you so perplexed that you skipped over them?

Here's why the situation can be baffling. Let's take the example of a

Customer Service Department. The goal, of course, is to provide a level of service that results in satisfied customers. But what's the final destination? How do you know when you're there?

If You Don't Know Where You're Going, Any Road Will Get You There

The final destination or Vision for any Customer Service Department is 100% customer satisfaction. Yet that can be frustrating because, based on human nature, it seems impossible to achieve. Nevertheless, that's where customer service managers worth their salt are leading departments.

Unrealistic? Sure. But that's the thing about destinations in the business world; they ARE unrealistic. Who could have envisioned Facebook, Apple, or Amazon? Could our great-grandparents have imagined flying to Europe, let alone the moon? Well, some visionaries did, and today the impossible becoming reality is no longer surprising.

So wherever you are leading your team, understand that if the destination is easily reached, it's not challenging enough for them to become engaged in its achievement. More than anything, **employee engagement means those on your team have opportunities every day to use the creative parts of their minds.** Their creative minds kick in when they have problems to solve, not when tasked with maintaining the status quo. So create a big challenge and watch your team flourish.

2. **Clearly communicate your goal/destination to your team.**

Tony Robbins, the world-class success coach, is famous for saying, "Repetition is the mother of mastery." And so it is. Continually communicating the goal/destination to your team in ways that get them ignited again and again marks a true leader. Assuming your people know the destination because you told them only once or twice does not work; it never will. *They will forget.* Heck, YOU and the rest of the leadership team forget half the time!

Using basketball teams as examples (I love basketball! I grew up cheering for my hometown Boston Celtics). You don't have to tell the players their goal is winning each game. They know that and commit to it 100%. What they're likely to forget is this: Meeting that goal does not guarantee they'll reach the ultimate destination of creating a world-class team capable of winning the top competition.

Just as championship basketball players have to be reminded to focus on more than the immediate game, a customer service department's destination of 100% customer satisfaction has to be reinforced continually.

So when the destination seems out of reach, how do you keep your team pointed in the right direction? By always "acting as if" you'll reach the destination. Motivation lies in repeatedly addressing the key questions in the box.

Questions to Answer: Who do we need to be and how do we need to behave to reach this destination? How can we keep the final destination uppermost in our minds as we go about our work each day?

Remember, you get more of what you focus on. If you can find clever ways to keep you and your team focused on where you're headed, the work won't only be more enjoyable; it will be more meaningful.

3. Using Socratic Delegation, solicit your team's input for how to get to the goal/destination.

Whaaaat? Ask my TEAM for input?!?

You already know the downside of command-and-control as a delegation tool (except in certain cases). In fact, it's not a tool at all; it's generally used as an attempt to control the uncontrollable—other people's actions.

Let's take the focus off your team for the moment and place it on you so you can fully grasp the problem with command-and-control leadership when trying to achieve your Mission. As established earlier, when your boss or a customer asks for a result for you to act on, what do people begin doing? (Remember, in their minds, they're already in full planning mode.) When you use command-and-control at unnecessary times, your team members, at best, hear only half of what you're saying. This is why command-and-control doesn't work. You could be incredibly expert at giving good directions, but it won't matter if team members don't hear what you're saying!

When you use Socratic Delegation instead and solicit their input, they will reveal their plans, and then you can work with them to fine-tune those plans. The $100,000 question then becomes: What is the likelihood the plans they came up with (and that you helped tweak) will be done as agreed upon? That's right. The chances fall north of 95% because the plans came from them in the first place. THAT is the strongest argument for soliciting their input for getting to the destination/goal.

If your people continually need specific instructions from you on what to do in their areas of responsibility, then your leadership needs work. The first step is to stop using command-and-control; it's not effective in the long run. (Have I hammered home this point enough? Is a cease-and-desist order really necessary?)

> "Give as few orders as possible," his father had told him once long ago. "Once you've given orders on a subject, you must always give orders on that subject."
>
> — Frank Herbert (from the novel *Dune*)

4. Become a walking, breathing scoreboard of measures.

When I managed marketing intelligence for a software company, every leader went through an annual 360° feedback process. An important piece of feedback I heard from my team was this: I was skilled at providing direction but terrible at letting them know what happened during the project and after it was complete.

From this I learned: (1) We all want to know where we stand in relation to each goal, and (2) we want to clearly understand the impact of our work on the whole organization.

And while all employees want to know where they stand, Millennials insist on it. If your leadership style is, "I told you once you're doing well. If that changes, I'll let you know," you likely have issues with your team's productivity and ownership of their work. Imagine a basketball game in which the rules were changed and, instead of revealing the score as the game unfolds, you don't find out who won until the game is over. That's what it feels like to your employees when you assign goals and don't let them know the score as they forge ahead.

Our society is deeply entrenched in keeping score, whether it's in sports, political polls, or competition-based reality shows. That's true in business, too.

It can be argued that employees should track for themselves where they stand in relation to a goal. That might be possible if the goal remains fixed. But you and I both know the goal/deliverables of nearly all projects get adapted as they move forward. What happens if we forget to pass along changes to those doing the work? They often end up working toward a goal that no longer exists. When that happens, people can become demotivated and less productive. This is a compelling reason for you to be a walking, breathing scoreboard.

Even if the goal remains fixed and your employees know where they stand, they want assurance that you agree with that self-assessment. When employees know you see their progress, they get more motivated.

In the *Harvard Business Review* article "The Power of Small Wins," Teresa Amabile and Steven J. Kramer, authors of *The Progress Principle*, emphasize how important seeing progress is:

By supporting people and their daily progress in meaningful work, managers improve not only the inner work lives of their employees but also the organization's long-term performance, which enhances inner work life even more. Of course, there is a dark side—the possibility of negative feedback loops. If managers fail to support progress and the people trying to make it, inner work life suffers and so does performance; and degraded performance further undermines inner work life.

When employees know where they stand in relation to the goals, then together you can determine where creativity is most needed. The more they apply their creativity, the more engaged they become.

"How Does What I Do Every Day Support the Mission?"

If you want your employees to partner with you in achieving the Mission, then clearly identify and articulate what role they play. Does the receptionist think answering phones is his only task? Does the mailroom clerk think she's only delivering mail? Or do they clearly understand—because of repeated reinforcement—that without their contributions, the Mission could not be accomplished? Do they know why that's true? Do you?

Although this works best if modeled from the top down, it doesn't need to be. If you are a manager or supervisor, you can apply this in your own department.

Start with your role and what it has to do with accomplishing the Mission. Work with your team members to identify the same for them. Then make the organization's Mission central to your department's culture, ensuring each person understands precisely where his or her contribution means something.

When Employees Could Care Less about the Mission

If someone on your team doesn't seem invested in the company's Mission, pull him or her aside and have a conversation that goes something like this: "This is what our company is all about, what we're trying to accomplish, and yet we don't see you participating. How can we get you moving toward the same goals?"

What if you've said and done everything right, yet your employee still isn't performing up to the required standards? Then it's time to stop investing your attention on a losing proposition.

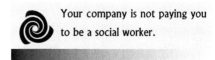

Your company is not paying you to be a social worker.

Over the years, I've been hired by many leaders to coach team members who need to increase their performance. My success rate is good but not 100%. Why? Because from time to time, individuals come to the coaching relationship hoping I have a magic formula that will do the hard work for them. I wish I did; I'd ingest it myself.

You cannot do for others what they're unwilling to do for themselves.

Here's a pithy rule that covers people who just don't want to do the work: Go to the ends of the earth for those who are doing the footwork (even if imperfectly) and walk away from those who are not.

Know and Support Your Employees' Personal Missions

Where else can you spend your leadership time and focus? Discover what people do well and, wherever possible, work with them to leverage their core competencies.

For more than 15 years, I've used an assessment tool called the Harrison Innerview to align people's passions with business results. This incredible tool gets to the heart of what people take pleasure in doing. The assumption is that, if you enjoy doing something, you'll be good at it—or at least be motivated to get good at it. Imagine the wonderful things that can occur when what each of your team members enjoys aligns beautifully with his/her job in terms of innovation, productivity, and efficiency.

The Harrison Innerview assesses what motivates the person taking the test. Compensation? A cause? Self-achievement? Knowing this can start a useful conversation that gets to your team member's personal Mission—what it is or could be.

Ways to Find Out Personal Missions

What other ways will help you gather knowledge about your team members' personal Missions? Consider these:

- Get to know them by using the Delegation Mind Meld discussed in Chapter 1.
- Observe what they do at work that goes beyond the scope of their jobs—on their breaks and at lunch, for example.
- Note what components of their lives they talk about with enthusiasm.
- Ask what non-related work expertise they have that might reveal their own missions and core competencies.
- Discuss what they do when they're not working.

By exploring, you might uncover a talent you were unaware of that can be put to use at your company. For example, does one team member enjoy coaching soccer? Maybe he's good at leading others to achieve a common goal, so you'd develop him with an eye toward management. To test this idea, you'd delegate a few projects that require leadership.

Do you have an employee who likes organizing family events—weddings, birthday parties, vacations? This person could become a future project manager, so assign her a small project and watch what she does with it.

Maybe someone in administration volunteers to help elderly people balance their checkbooks. Might she belong in an accounting role? Could you ask her to help you with financial reports so you can see her capabilities?

Okay, I don't know what you can do with an employee who volunteers as a clown for kids' parties and has a talent for making balloon animals. Don't expect me to supply all the answers! But maybe that person can help you set up work as a game and introduce fun!

Achieve Your Mission by Turning It into a Game

As mentioned earlier in "Why You Should Read This Book," a recent Gallup Poll revealed that 70% of employees are disengaged (and 65% of the leadership team!). Yet, as you read this, millions of people all over the world engage in role-plays on the Internet. Yes, if you play any sort of game electronically, you are a gamer—and computer solitaire counts, although barely. (I once heard a comic say, "I just bought a computer. Basically, it's a $1,000 deck of cards!")

Gaming is a multibillion-dollar industry! What does it mean when people prefer make-believe to reality? And why create an artificial game when life itself is so challenging?

Please don't misunderstand. I don't think there's anything wrong with gaming; it serves a purpose and can be loads of fun. I also know many people hide out wasting precious time playing electronic games as a way to avoid important issues in their lives. Here's the irony:

Everything Gamers Want in Artificial Games Can Be Found at Work!

Note the components of any game:

- A clear goal with obstacles to achieving it. Excitement and fun come in finding ways to get around the obstacles.
- As part of your strategy, you assume an identity you believe will produce the desired results.
- You figure out who among the players can be useful to you—that is, has complementary objectives—and those who go against you because of opposing objectives.

Your people WANT to be challenged, but they also want to feel they have a say in how they play the game.

- You succeed at the game to the extent that you can keep your objectives clearly in mind and develop workable strategies to achieve them.

- Sometimes you win and sometimes you lose.
- There's always another game to play.

What a great description of WORK!

Die-hard gamers welcome the difficulty of the games they play—the more difficult the better. Victory feels sweeter when you've faced obstacles and found your way around them. If that's true in gaming, it can also be applied at work.

I dream that, one day, all people have work they enjoy so much, they say, "Thank God it's Monday!" (Okay, stop laughing; it's possible!) To get there requires embracing the reality of day-to-day life and figuring out ways to make it so interesting, you don't need artificial games to have a good time.

Here's how to inspire your team members to set up work as a game:

- **When you delegate, give them a goal of beating their personal best**. If they've always achieved an objective within a certain time frame, see how much time they can shave off of it. If their accuracy or quality is around 80%, challenge them to increase it.

- **Encourage them to develop better methods and different strategies.** Just because something has always worked doesn't mean a better way can't be found. Encourage them to try improving their methods and strategies.

- **Challenge them to find the lazy way.** Laziness is responsible for many of the greatest inventions of all time. (Think of the TV remote control or the microwave oven.) How would a lazy person approach this work? Are people making the work more difficult than it need be? Are you?

- **Ask them to achieve even better results**. Maybe they're already "lazy" and have found ways to do the least amount of work while achieving desired results. How can you create a game with the objective of achieving better results in the same time and with the same amount of effort?

- **Have a contest for the best game**. After you've introduced this "work as a game" concept to them, have them develop games of their own. Encourage them to let their minds wander into strategy mode. Invite them to let their imaginations run free. Give prizes for categories such as most ingenious, most effective, best results, and so on.

- **Have a scoreboard**. People enjoy seeing where the team stands. And remember, you should become a "walking, breathing scoreboard." Having one displayed on the wall or on everyone's computer screen (or both) makes the game more real and more inspiring!

Lessons from the Apollo 11 Mission

Years ago, I read *Peak Performers* by Dr. Charles Garfield. He was inspired to write this book by what he witnessed working on the Apollo 11 Mission to put a man on the moon. Garfield saw mediocre workers turn into extraordinary ones because the Mission ignited their passion.

He also saw them return to mediocrity when the quest was accomplished.

Intrigued, Garfield set out on his own 20-year Mission to discover what separates peak performers from everyone else. His most overarching concept: ***Top performers have a motivating Mission.***

Now, apply that concept to your organization. Do your employees have to scour your company's website for its Mission Statement? Do you?

Start with insisting every one of your employees, leaders, board directors, and you know the Mission Statement by heart. Ideally, every meeting would begin with a recitation of the Mission Statement. Every strategy, every project plan, and every task you delegate would clearly delineate how it helps accomplish the Mission. Every company email would have the Mission Statement at the bottom. Tony Robbins is correct: "Repetition is the mother of mastery."

Remember the Apollo 11 Mission. Even if your company doesn't shoot for something as exciting as the landing on the moon, your work is important.

Put Your Mission in Constant Focus Because you get more of what you focus on, ensure every team member is constantly focused on your Mission.

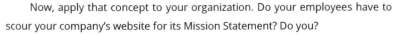

When all team members fully understand each of their roles in achieving it, employee engagement will increase significantly.

Conclusion ->

Every successful endeavor began with a Mission, whether it's the Apollo 11 Mission to land on the moon or to bring a product to market. When you and your team have clarity about where you're going and the role you play in achieving your organization's Mission, the result is more innovation and more creativity. You can literally turn work into a game more satisfying than most.

> "If you want to build a ship, don't drum up the men to gather wood, divide the work, and give orders. Instead, teach them to yearn for the vast and endless sea."
> — Antoine de Saint-Exupery

Use Socratic Delegation to gain their input on how to win the game and consistently achieve your Mission. Be a walking, talking scoreboard and the result will be more engagement and, yes, more fun!

---

i http://www.gallup.com/poll/189071/little-change-employee-engagement-january.aspx
ii Teresa Amabile and Steven J. Kramer, "The Power of Small Wins," Harvard Business Review, May 2011.

CHAPTER 6: THE ROLE OF SOCRATIC DELEGATION IN EMPLOYEE ENGAGEMENT

This book responds to an escalating crisis in the workplace. Employees (including managers) are less and less invested in the work they do and the outcomes they deliver. This non-specific malaise is costing them dearly and the businesses that employ them (as noted in Why You Should Read This Book).

The financial cost to employees is equally profound, though less well researched. It shows up in lost opportunities, stalled careers, and insufficient salaries to make ends meet (let alone pay off staggering amounts of education debt). Imagine the effect on morale when your employees are looking down the road without hope for improvement.

Learning how to delegate well can have a positive impact on your company's bottom line through increased employee engagement. Not only that, it will also provide better opportunities for those employees, once asleep at the wheel, who wake up to become invested in the company and their own careers. It is an act of service for those whose careers you hold in your hands.

Socratic Delegation =
Empowerment = Engagement

Poor Delegation =
Discouragement = Disengagement

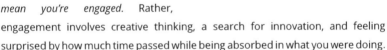

Merely doing your job doesn't mean you're engaged. Rather, engagement involves creative thinking, a search for innovation, and feeling surprised by how much time passed while being absorbed in what you were doing.

And that's possible at any level—whether you're part of the executive team, a server at a restaurant, or a janitor of a building. It's not about what you're doing; it's about how you feel while doing it.

Although you cannot force

Your job as a leader is to remove obstacles that stand in the way of your people getting their jobs done well.

employees to engage without their cooperation, you can create a culture fertile for engagement to happen.

Obstacles in the Way of Delegating

Related to delegation, which of the following obstacles might be standing in the way of your team getting the job done?

- Unclear outcomes
- Outcomes impossible to measure
- Deadlines not communicated clearly
- Deadlines that are unrealistic or impossible to meet
- Changing the expected outcome or deadline

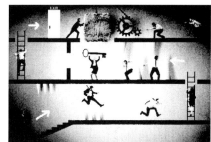

Using the processes in this book will go a long way toward eliminating those obstacles to engagement.

The Hidden Costs of Low Employee Engagement

How is your organization affect by its leaders' lack of delegation skills? Here are five possibilities:

1. You won't be able to attract and hire the top talent.
2. Your employees will leave—usually the best ones first.
3. Process improvements stall.
4. Your organization's productivity levels go down and so do your revenues.
5. You miss opportunities to develop your team members and their potential value.

Let's discuss each of them:

1. You won't be able to attract and hire the top talent.

In this age of over-communication, if your company has lackluster leadership and widespread employee disengagement, it quickly and pervasively becomes well known within your industry. Although you may be able to hire people, you won't attract the most talented because they have options. They strategically choose the companies they work for with an eye toward enhancing their personal résumés. Your company's reputation will be strongly considered when they make career decisions.

2. Your employees will leave—usually the best ones first.

How many millions of dollars have been spent by organizations to retain the best of the best? Is it working in your company? While benefits and perks might keep you competitive, in the end, retention boils down to employee engagement, and THAT often boils down to the individual's immediate supervisor. Consider this evidence: Experts conservatively estimate the cost to find and train an employee's replacement as one and a half to more than twice a staffer's annual salary.

This is due to:

- Reduced productivity
- Organizational wisdom that walks out the door with the employee
- Time taken up by management and Human Resources to hire a replacement
- Overworked and stressed staff covering the responsibilities of those who left
- Expenses related to training the replacement
- Direct costs of hiring (e.g., advertising and recruiter fees)

3. Process improvements stall.

In organizations where engagement is low, work processes quickly become stale and outdated. Employees who work daily with various systems that get the work product out the door know what's working and what's not. Typically, they

discuss among themselves how things could be done better and quicker. However, if the management team doesn't accept that employees have good ideas to contribute or are too busy to ask, then improving processes depends on:

- the limited time managers have to devote to it,
- the limited experience those same managers have with the processes sorely in need of improvement, or

(3) hiring expensive consultants.

4. Your organization's productivity levels go down and so do your revenues.

Every leader should take time to ponder this question: *Why don't we have the time to clearly delegate tasks and projects at the beginning, but we always have time to clean up the mess when they aren't done properly?*

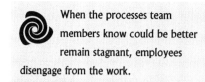

When the processes team members know could be better remain stagnant, employees disengage from the work.

Take a look at the "do overs" within your area of responsibility and trace their root causes. Often mistakes are made for these reasons:

- The person delegating the task or project hasn't clearly defined the expectations and required results.
- The person taking on the task didn't have all the information required to do the job and didn't feel engaged in the process.

Far too many managers say, "My employees will come to me if they have questions." Please believe that no matter how good your relationship is with them, most people are reluctant to voluntarily display their lack of knowledge, especially to their boss. As a leader, it's your job to extract those questions from them using Socratic Delegation.

5. You will miss opportunities to develop your team members and their potential value.

Within the delegation of every task or project is an opportunity to further develop the skills of the employee to whom you are delegating. When a leader spends time at the front end discussing how to achieve the required result, opportunities to uncover any gaps in the employee's skills and knowledge emerge. So do opportunities to provide coaching on how to achieve the result more efficiently. The knowledge acquired enhances the employee's capabilities and career potential moving forward.

The immediate supervisor has the most impact on an employee's desire to perform.

Common Misconceptions about Employee Engagement

How do people tend to think about engagement in incorrect ways? Here are three common misconceptions.

MISCONCEPTION #1 – Employee engagement is just another term for coddling employees.

I am not asking you to coddle your team; I'm asking you to do what works!

Are you living in the past, still trying to use the command-and-control style of management when it's no longer relevant? Ironically, using this old-fashioned style DOES coddle employees. It treats them like small children who need to be told what to do step by step!

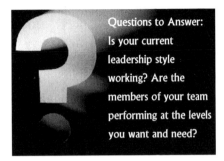

Questions to Answer: Is your current leadership style working? Are the members of your team performing at the levels you want and need?

MISCONCEPTION #2 – I manage to be engaged without any external motivation; why can't others do the same?

Let me challenge that assertion by asking, "ARE you engaged? Really?"

• When was the last time you came up with a more efficient way for you or your team to get work done?

• What's the last project you couldn't wait to sink your teeth into?

• How often do you count the days to the weekend? To vacation? To retirement?

MISCONCEPTION #3 – Some employees just don't want to be engaged.

Imagine you're on a television game show. Two doors stand in front of you, and you have to choose one.

Door #1 – a job in which you're routinely asked for input on how to produce desired results and given feedback that supports your growth

Door #2 – a job in which you're routinely told what to do and how to do it. You get no consideration for presenting a better way, and you're given no feedback or "constructive criticism."

Do you sincerely believe any employees would choose Door #2? They would have to be people who have accepted they don't think for themselves and want to continually be told what to do.

If you ask, "Tell me about the best boss you ever had," how often do you think employees would describe a boss who gave them orders, breathed down their necks until completing the task, and then told them how they'd done it wrong? If that seems harsh to you, you likely don't fit that description.

If your management style consistently produces phenomenal results, I applaud you. If, however, you think you have "more to go," then use the processes and tools in this book to figure out how to get you and your team more engaged and thus more productive.

Practice Makes Perfect!

Merely reading this book will not make you a better delegator. (You respond, "Now, why didn't you mention that at the beginning?")

Getting good at delegating is like everything else—it takes practice, DAILY practice. Savvy leaders know this and often use the services of a coach to help them transition into this new style of delegating. They understand that, left to their own devices, they will quickly forget what they've learned and slip back into their familiar practices.

 Delegation is a core competency that, once mastered, will make you one of a few who are true leaders versus one of the many who simply hand out assignments.

Companies that want to incorporate these practices across the organization will only succeed if they create a long-term program (six months minimum; 12 months is better). Every month, groups of six to eight leaders meet to discuss how they're applying these processes. Sharing challenges with the rest of the group helps everyone come up with better ways to practice these new behaviors. And hearing success stories inspires them to keep going.

Groups could be facilitated by an outside consultant ("Hi, my name is Silver.") or a skilled inside facilitator such as one of your Human Resources professionals. You could even model the group after a book club— that is, you'd take a section of this book each month and discuss how you're applying the concepts in your department. Most important, though, is meeting monthly to maintain

forward momentum. Without consistent support, practicing the principles in this book will be much more difficult.

As an authority figure, you have many opportunities to use your influence for good. Building influence requires mutual respect between you and those you want to lead. You build this respect by fully delegating—that is, allowing your team to support you as you let go of the belief that you have to micro-manage everything.

 2016 Corporate Culture Study % of low level employees who make independent decisions:

Always	4%
Usually	16%
Sometimes	63%
Never	18%

Practicing Socratic Delegation itself supports you in having more influence over the results of your team. When you ask good questions and stop talking, you collaborate with your team instead of being their overseer. That means letting team members have more control over how they do their jobs, and clearly conveying how their performance is being evaluated for each assignment.

That gives them confidence.

Step away so they can do more problem solving. Eventually, you'll happily turn off your cell phone when you go on vacation, knowing all will be fine.

Command-and-control works well in military-style organizations and even then only when danger is imminent. Great military leaders reveal they only gained significant influence over their troops after gaining their respect. That says those stars and bars will only go so far and no further. Just ask Captain Bligh whose naval crew, having had enough of his cruel command, set him and his loyalists adrift in a lifeboat—a story famously told in the novel and movie *Mutiny on the Bounty*.

When it comes to gaining influence through thoughtful and clear delegation, the quickest way to affect change is using the Socratic Delegation process.

Conclusion ->

Employee disengagement is costing your organization dearly. The toll it takes is often invisible. Eventually, it shows up in less profitability and lost opportunities to develop employees who can grow the company in unforeseen ways.

Practicing Socratic Delegation uncorks potential. It gives your organization the means to build a reputation that attracts and keeps top talent. It provides access to

"The greatest good you can do for another is not just share your riches, but to reveal to him his own."
— Benjamin Disraeli

ideas for process improvements from those on the front line. And, as employees become more engaged, so will the customers you serve, creating a quadruple win: you, the organization, the employees, and those you serve.

If the potential for that makes your rub your hands together in excited anticipation, then you are a born leader!

FINAL THOUGHTS

Leading others is an art and a privilege. It is also one of the most difficult roles you will play—whether you're leading a team at work or parenting your own children. You can't go wrong if you lead with love, kindness, and a spirit of service.

It's my greatest wish that the concepts in this book will serve you and those you lead. If ever I can be of support in your work, please reach out.

The Socratic Delegation Process Step-by-Step (repeated in the next section for convenient reference) is the foundational process that will serve you well. However, depending on the size or scope of the task or project, you will likely need to dig deeper. In the next section, you will find a supplemental list of questions, Deeper Socratic Delegation, to assist you.

Finally, although this book was written for those in paid management positions, it has application beyond that. These concepts have been tried and proven useful for event planners, teachers, parents, and those who manage volunteers. Again, Socratic Delegation is the foundation; in the next section, you will find questions for Project Managers that will also be useful.

> "I've learned that people will forget what you said, people will forget what you did, but people will never forget how you made them feel."
> — Maya Angelou

Silver Rose

LISTS OF QUESTIONS

THE ~~Incredibly Useful~~ SOCRATIC DELEGATION PROCESS
STEP-BY-STEP

Step #1 - Identify the task or project.

Step #2 - Clearly state the measurable results/outcomes and timeframe. (By the way, this is often the culprit of problems. If you don't clearly define how to measure success, how is the person to whom you are delegating supposed to know?)

Step #3 - Meet with the individual or team to whom you are delegating and have the following conversation:

- "Here's an overview of the work and why it needs to be done." The why of what you're delegating is very important. People are more likely to become engaged in their work if they know why they're doing it. Millennials in particular want to understand why.

- "Here is the result needed and the date we need it: _____."

- "Would you walk me through how you think it should be done?" OR "How do you think we should approach this?"

- Listen and only listen until the end. Take notes so you remember the agreements made.

- Don't interrupt; if you identify a problem and stop to mention it, you may interrupt the person's thought process. Also, it's likely s/he will, while talking through the task, identify the very problem you noticed and address it directly—the ideal scenario.

Step # 4 - Fine-tune

- If you noticed any potential concerns while the plans were being outlined, bring them up by asking questions:

◊ How will you get to that point?

◊ Where are those resources coming from?

◊ Help me understand _____

◊ What tools are you planning to use?

◊ What obstacles might stand in the way of getting this done on time?

◊ And so on.

- This fine-tuning process is your opportunity to coach the individual to a higher level of skill and strategizing.

- This is also an opportunity for you to learn approaches you hadn't thought of yourself.

- It gives you a perfect chance to acknowledge the team or individual for thinking critically.

- Before delegating to any member of your team, be certain YOU are clear about Steps 1 and 2:

  1. Identify the task or project, and
  2. Clearly state the measurable results/outcomes and timeframe.

Each step is critical to achieving success.

For a PDF of the Socratic Delegation Process, go to:
http://www.DelegateForResults.com/SocraticDelegationProcess

Deeper Socratic Delegation

Note: some of these questions are repetitive so you can choose how you want to ask them. If you ask the same question in two different ways, you may get more information the second time around.

WHO

- Who asked for this?
- Who is/are the right ones to do this?
- Who will spearhead the project?
- Who are the stakeholders?
- Who is responsible for each milestone and what are the dates for each?
- Who is our customer?
- Who is our audience?
- Who should we share this information with? Who else needs to be involved?
- From whom do you need information or other key elements in order to complete this?
- Manager/Supervisor: What role do you want me to play as you are doing this?

WHAT

- What's at stake with this project?
- What will it be used for?
- What's the strategy?
  - Objectives?
  - Goals?
- Imagine there's a headline in the local newspaper about the results at the end of this project. What would you want it to read?
- What could we learn from doing this?
- What excites you about this task/ project?
- What are the hidden agendas we need to know about?
- What is the measurement of success, internally and externally?
- What is the measurable result you want to produce?
- What criteria should we use to determine the success of this project?
- What milestones will you use to track progress?
- What is the timeline?
- What is your deadline?
- What are your ideas/ suggestions?
- What could stand in the way of getting it done?

> This is an opportunity for the employee to remind you she has a two-week vacation scheduled in the middle of the project. Without asking the question, the employee often assumes you remember and have already taken it into consideration. The truth is, it may very well have slipped your mind, and it's a good thing she reminded you!

Deeper Socratic Delegation (Continued)

WHAT (cont'd)

- What problems do you anticipate?
- What's the solution/prevention?
- What's the budget?
- What priority does this have within the big picture?
- What do you think the first step should be?
- What do you think the next step should be?
- What resources do you have to accomplish this?

- What's your strategy?
- What resources will you need to accomplish this?
- What will it look like when it's done?
- What's the most efficient way to do this?
- What obstacles might you encounter?
- What's your plan if you encounter obstacles?
- What could prevent you from completing this on time?
- What's possible?

WHERE

- Where does this fall within YOUR work priorities?
- Where will you get your cost information?
- Where will we find the resources we need?

WHY

- Why does this need to be done?
- What will it take for you to be on board?
- What reservations do you have?
- Would you want to work on this if you didn't have to? Why?

HOW

- How would you approach this?
- How does this fit into your current workload?
- How does this impact other projects/activities?
- How will it be perceived by others?
- How would you approach this if you knew you couldn't fail?
- How will you know when you've accomplished this?
- How will you keep me informed of the status?
- How does this assignment impact your existing workload?
- How will we share the information on this project before, during and after?
- How will we celebrate when it's completed?

WRAP-UP

- What haven't we covered that we should?
- If there were one big question in your mind about (topic under discussion), what would it be?
- Can we count on you? (Ask each person individually.)

Some *Incredibly Useful* Project Management Questions

WHO

- Who requested this?
- Who is our customer?
- Who is our audience?
- Whose authorization do we need for the various components?
- Who is/are the right ones to do this?
- Who will spearhead the project?
- Who needs to be on the project team?
- Who are the stakeholders?

- Who owns each milestone?
- Who are our champions within the organization and how can we best utilize their support?
- Who are the naysayers within the organization and how can they hurt our progress?
- Who should we share this information with? Who else needs to be involved?
- From whom do we need information or other key elements in order to complete this?

WHAT

- What's at stake with this project?
- What will it be used for?
- What's the strategy?
    - Objectives?
    - Goals?
- What are the milestones?
- If there were a headline on our website at the end of this project, what would we want it to read?
- What could we learn from doing this?
- What excites us about this task/project?
- What are the hidden agendas we need to know about?
- What is the measurement of success, internally and externally?
- What is the measurable result?
- What knowledge do we need to acquire to do this?
- What is the timeline?
- What criteria should we use to determine the success of this project?

- What milestones will we use to track progress?
- What are some ideas/ suggestions?
- What could stand in the way of getting it done? What problems do we anticipate?
    - What are solutions/ preventions?
- What's the budget?
- What priority does this have within the big picture?
- What do we think the first step should be?
- What should the next step be?
- What resources do we already have to accomplish this?
- What resources will we need to accomplish this?
- What will it look like when it's done?
- What's the most efficient way to do this?
- What obstacles might we encounter?
    - What's our plan to overcome each?

Some ~Incredibly Useful~ Project Management Questions (Continued)

- What could prevent us from completing this on time?
- What's our strategy?
- What will it take for each of us to be on board?
- What reservations do we have?
- What's possible?

WHEN

- When is the final project due?
- When is each milestone due?
- When do we need to order each resource to get it here on time?
- When do we need to provide updates?
- When are vacations/days off scheduled and how will that impact our deadline?

WHERE

- Where does this fall within our work priorities?
- Where will we get cost information?
- Where will we find the resources we need?

WHY

- Why does this need to be done?
- Would we want to work on this if we didn't have to? Why?

HOW

- How will we track progress?
- How does this fit into our current workload?
- How does this impact other projects/activities?
- How will others perceive this?
- How would we approach this if we knew we couldn't fail?
- How will we know when we've accomplished this?
- How will we keep each other informed of the status?
- How does this assignment impact each individual's workload?
- How will we share the information on this project before, during and after?
- How will we celebrate when it's completed?
- How can we cushion ourselves against unanticipated illness or other events that impact progress?

WRAP-UP

- What haven't we covered that we should?
- If there were one big question in your mind about (topic under discussion), what would it be?
- Can we count on you? (Ask each person individually.)

"The best minute you spend is the one you invest in people."

- Kenneth H. Blanchard

RESOURCES

The Gallup Organization www.Gallup.com/topic/employee_engagement.aspx

The Progress Principle
Using Small Wins to Ignite Joy, Engagement, and Creativity at Work
by Teresa Amabile & Steven Kramer
Harvard Business Review Press

The Thin Book of Appreciative Inquiry
by Sue Annis Hammond
Thin Book Publishing Company

The One Minute Manager
By Kenneth Blanchard, Ph.D. and Spencer Johnson, M.D.
Berkley Books

DRIVE
The Surprising Truth about What Motivates Us
By Daniel H. Pink
Riverhead Books

The Art of Focused Conversation
100 Ways to Access Group Wisdom in the Workplace
General Editor: R. Brian Stanfield
New Society Publishers

"If you spent $75,000 on a piece of capital equipment, you would make sure you invested time and money to maintain it so you get the appropriate ROI. Are you doing the same with your human capital?"

- Silver Rose

About the Author

The Story: Silver Rose was born and grew up in Boston. She went to San Diego City College, majoring in journalism. When her family moved to Nevada, she joined them and began her meteoric career. She was administrative assistant to the governor of Nevada at 23. At age 25, she owned an insurance agency and was selected as one of the Outstanding Young Women of America. She was then recruited by a British media tycoon to be his second in command, including serving as creative director and head of sales. For the next 20 years, she worked in the computer industry where her specialties were human resources, sales, and marketing. Her management positions included manager of sales database, manager of marketing intelligence, and vice president of sales and marketing.

For the last decade, Silver has been a professional speaker, heading her own management consulting and executive coaching practice.

The Style: After more than 100 standup comedy club performances, Silver has learned to take her work seriously but not herself. Drawing on her vast experience, she approaches serious subjects with a light touch. She immediately connects with audience members, talking with them and not at them in a relaxed, fun, and style. They leave feeling upbeat and good about themselves.

Silver has worked with an impressive list of both public and private sector organizations across the country. She started writing an online column long before they were called blogs. Today, she continues to perform stand-up comedy, has three published books, and won the highest achievement award given by the Dale Carnegie organization. However, her proudest achievement is having successfully raised her two "at risk" daughters whom she adopted from foster care at the ages of 12 and 15.

Examples of Clients: Bristol Myers Squibb, Farmers Insurance, Hilton Hotels, Raymond James, Kaiser Permanente, Hilton Hotels, Security Title, Trinity Health, Association of Practice Managers, UC Davis, State of Maryland, City of Tempe, Veterans Administration, and numerous workforce development organizations across the United States.

Silver's 3 Most Requested Programs

- Getting Others to WILLINGLY Do What Needs to be Done!
- Delegation, Feedback, & Laughter in the Workplace: *Increasing Employee Engagement*
- Lighten Up & Lead – *Re-engaging Employees*

Testimonials:

"Your style was terrific. You tailored your program to the interests of the group and were up to date with our industry. Thank you again for the OUTSTANDING program."

Alicia Valencia Erb, CUDE
American Association of Credit Union Leagues

I have had the opportunity to try your delegation technique a couple of times since your presentation and I like the way it works. The first person was a bit surprised and wasn't sure how to address my questions about her plans to best complete the work. After I let her think for a bit, she came up with some awesome, very helpful plans.

John Oberdiek,
Sr. Project Manager, Portland, OR

"You always invest the time and attention to deliver a message that is "spot on"! There's nobody like you!"

Barbara Willis, VP & State Counsel
Fidelity National Title Group

"YOU HIT IT OUT OF THE PARK! We asked you to put something together that would motivate our sales team and you over-delivered. Not only did you motivate them to improve, you showed them in precise detail how to do so. Your style was terrific: with humor, high energy, stories and excellent delivery. You tailored your program to the interests of the group and were up to date with recent changes in our industry. You were a true professional."

Ned Fajkowski, President
Security Title Agency

"The problem with being a leader is that you're never sure if you're being followed or chased."

- Claire A. Murray

HOW TO CONTACT SILVER ROSE

Silver Rose Enterprises, LLC
Keynotes, Workshops, Consulting & Executive Coaching
7000 N 16th Street #120-277
Phoenix, AZ 85020-5524
877-840-5416
info@SilverSpeaks.com
www.DelegateForResults.com

"Leadership has been defined as the ability to hide your panic from others."

- Lao Tzu

NOTES

NOTES

NOTES

NOTES